COUNTRIES OF TODAY

# East Africa

## Kenya, Uganda and Tanzania

C. P. KIRBY

ERNEST BENN LIMITED · LONDON

First published 1968 by Ernest Benn Limited
Bouverie House, Fleet Street, London, E.C.4

© C. P. Kirby 1968

Distributed in Canada by
The General Publishing Company Limited, Toronto

Printed in Great Britain

510–10701–X

# Contents

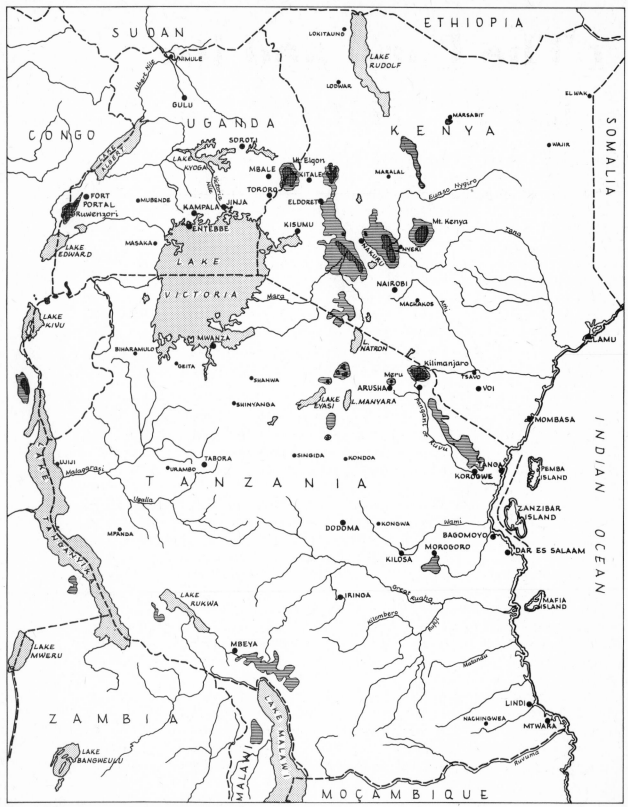

East Africa: Kenya, Uganda, Tanzania

# 1 The Land and its Early History

THE NAME 'EAST AFRICA' has come to be applied to a relatively small portion of the eastern part of Africa. The part is, however, a geographic whole, surrounded by physical features that have acted as boundaries since long before there were any political divisions of the land. To the east the Indian Ocean, to the south the Ruvuma River, to the west the great crescent of lakes, to the north the desert; these are the barriers that have contained East Africa, giving it an identity separate and distinct from the Sudan and Ethiopia to the north, the Congo forest to the west and, to a lesser extent, Zambia and Malawi to the south. The area within these boundaries is approximately 683,000 square miles and of this about 39,000 square miles are inland water. So although we have called this a small part of Africa, it is still an extremely large tract of land, over seven times as big as Great Britain. The distance from the Ruvuma River to the northern tip of Lake Rudolf is the same as the distance from London to the 'toe' of Italy; the coast is as far from the Ruwenzori Mountains as Edinburgh from Geneva. In this vast area live $25\frac{1}{2}$ million people of whom 25 million are Africans.

The flat coastal strip of land is about thirty miles wide, then the country rises in a tilted slab to a height of nearly 7,000 feet at the western boundary. This slab is cut by the great fault system called the Rift Valley and further dissected by the main river systems. Within our boundary lies the continental watershed (some of the rivers flowing to the Atlantic, some to the Mediterranean, some to the Indian Ocean) and in the centre there is an area of internal drainage where the rivers flow into lakes and swamps from which the water is lost by evaporation.

Along certain lines of weakness on the earth's crust subterranean forces have acted either to raise or lower the crust along the line of the fault. When there are two such faults running parallel to each other a valley is formed with steep sides called escarpments. The Great Rift Valley is just such a system. It starts near Beira in Portuguese East Africa and strikes northward to encompass Lake Malawi; north of the lake it splits into a 'Y', the western arm of which curls round into the trough that contains the chain of lakes that form the western boundary of the area we are dealing with, whilst the eastern arm stretches to the Red Sea, made by the Indian Ocean flooding into the cleft in the earth's surface. These huge furrows across the land have sides over 2,000 feet high and Lake Tanganyika, which lies in the western trough, has a depth of water of 4,700 feet, making it the world's second deepest lake.

The terrific forces warping the earth's crust along the fault lines of the Rift have also weakened the crust in many other places, both within the Valley and along the edges. At these points of weakness the boiling rock forces itself through the crust, erupting to the surface in volcanoes, most of which are long dead, but some of which are still active. These eruptions were of two kinds and have left behind two different types of mountain. When the weakness was in one spot the rock formed a large cone round the single vent through which the lava flowed. With weathering and erosion this cone becomes a dome with the hardest part of the rock (the 'plug' of molten rock solidified in the old vent) standing above the dome as a rocky peak. Mount Kenya is a typical example of a volcanic plug left perched on a weathered base, but there are many other old volcanoes with their crater walls still standing. When the weakness was a crack in the earth's surface the molten rock forced itself out as a long ridge, the weathering of which produced ranges of mountains such as the Aberdares and the Mau. Kilimanjaro is particularly interesting, for on one 'base' there are three volcanoes of very different ages. Kibo, the snowy dome (19,340 feet), is a perfect crater that is still slightly active, emitting sulphurous steam; Mawenzi (17,564 feet), the south-eastern peak, is the plug of a much older volcano, eroded to a pile of crumbling rock; and Shira (13,140 feet), which lies to the north-west, still retains the vestiges of a crater wall.

The physical features of the land provide the bones of the landscape but the flesh is dependent upon the climate. To make farming possible in East Africa there must be a rainfall of thirty inches per year, and for cattle ranching at least twenty inches per year are necessary. Judged by these standards most of East Africa is very deficient in rainfall. There are, however, two areas where such rainfall does generally occur: the coastal strip with the direct benefit of the monsoon winds of the Indian Ocean and the area of highlands and inland lakes where the water evaporated from the surface of the lakes is condensed by the mountains and falls as rain, to drain back to the lakes again through the rivers. Because of this rainfall pattern there is a very high population density along the coast and the shores of the lakes.

Along the coast mangrove swamps alternate with coconut plantations. Then there is a great strip of dry dusty savannah grassland, with *Acacia* thorn trees and bushes. In the

1 The Rift Valley looking south. The two edges of the trough are marked by the clouds. In the background can be seen Kilimanjaro with its three separate volcanic cones: left, Mawenzi; centre, Kibo; right Shira

2 Mount Kenya. The photograph shows the formation of the mountain from the old volcanic 'plug'

north this savannah becomes true desert; in the centre it becomes the heavily cultivated area round Lake Victoria; while in the south it gives way to a vast tract of *miombo*, a fairly dense woodland heavily infested with tsetse fly. Out of these main vegetation areas rise the mountain masses, supporting a dense farming population and creating their own micro-climate, islands of green in a predominantly dry yellow landscape.

Next to the lack of rainfall, the tsetse fly is responsible for the sterilisation of the largest part of the land. Ten per cent of Kenya, thirty-two per cent of Uganda and sixty per cent of Tanganyika are infested with the various forms of this fly which can infect both men and cattle with *trypanosomiasis* or 'sleeping sickness'.

There is one other feature of East Africa that is world famous and which must be taken into account when describing the land: its wealth of wild life. In no other part of the world is there such a diversity of animals. On the plains vast herds of zebra, wildebeeste and kongoni graze the dry grasses, with gazelles and giraffes in smaller bands amongst them. In the forests and highlands there are buffalo and elephant, in the lakes hippopotamus and crocodile. The swift cheetah, the sly leopard and the lordly lion are spread throughout the country as is the short-sighted and irritable rhinoceros. In no other country has there been the same close contact between human and animal for so long. Until comparatively recently man co-existed with the animals in Africa, hunting them for meat and hides but not having any appreciable effect on their numbers. His herds shared the same grassland and often the same waterholes. Even the ivory hunting of the Arabs does not seem to have had any effect on the numbers of elephant. This traditional balance has now been upset by the coming of the 'sporting' hunter who shoots for pleasure and not subsistence, and the poacher who kills for profit. Already the pressures of civilisation are being felt, for although some of the

7

3 A fine old tusker in the Tsavo National Park

finest game country in the territory has been made into Reserves where no hunting is allowed, there are other areas where human occupation has had to be given priority and in which the game must take a subsidiary role. The balancing of the tourist potential of wild-life conservation with the demands for land of an expanding economy is going to be one of the really basic problems that the new East African countries will have to face.

In East Africa we can trace man back to his very earliest beginnings. The wealth of its archaeological sites makes it the focal point for all those who study the evolution of man. On Rusinga Island, in Lake Victoria, Dr Louis Leakey has discovered one of man's ances-tors – the ape-like creature named *Proconsul* – in fossil beds that have been dated as twenty-five million years old. Although he walked erect and lived wholly on the ground *Proconsul* was not, however, man. The point when true man emerges from his animal ancestors is generally defined as the moment when the animal starts to make tools to a set and regular pattern. Several animals use tools of a kind: gorillas use sticks to grub for roots, baboons often use stones to crush scorpions; but they never shape these tools specifically for the work they have to do. They use whatever is to hand, and thus are still animals by definition. It is *Zinjanthropus*, nicknamed 'Nut Cracker Man', and *Homo habilis* (Handy Man), found in beds just under two million years old in the Olduvai Gorge in Tanganyika, who are generally recognised as being the earliest men.

The Olduvai Gorge was discovered accidentally in 1911 by a German professor called Kattwinkel, who had come to Tanganyika (then known as German East Africa) to collect insects for the Berlin Museum. He was chasing a rare butterfly over the Serengeti plains when he nearly fell over the lip of a deep chasm that cut through the flat plain. When he scrambled down the cliff he found many fossil bones sticking out of the rock face and more bones littered at the foot.

When the bones were examined in Berlin it was realised that this Gorge was one of the most important archaeological sites in the world. Usually, a site relates to only one geological period, and it is sometimes very difficult to relate to the same time-scale a site in one place with others found elsewhere. At Olduvai there are two million years of evolution piled in layers, one on top of the other, so that the correct chronology can be seen immediately. We can follow the gradual improvement in tools, from *Homo habilis*' primitive split pebbles to the large 'hand axes' of the early Stone Age, and at the same time, relate these tools to the animals that lived during each age. In the earliest beds there are bones of strange extinct creatures like the *Metaschizotherium*, which was a giant antelope with claws instead of hooves, and the *Sivatherium*, which was a short-necked giraffe with antlers like a moose. In the later beds the species become more gigantic. Porcupines as big as Alsatians, pigs as large as rhinoceroses and wild sheep the size of ponies. Then in the latest beds there are animals once again of more normal size. In all the time covered by the Olduvai strata there is no sign of fire. Man was a hunter, but, like the animals he hunted, he ate his food raw and lived at the mercy of the elements.

Since 1931 Olduvai Gorge has been systematically explored by Dr Louis Leakey and his wife, but it was not until 1959 that they found the first skull, shattered into nearly 400 pieces, embedded in the cliff face. The skull proved to be of an ape-man with huge jaws and a ridge along the top of his skull to hold the muscles for the jaw. This species was named *Zinjanthropus*, and for some time was thought to be the maker of all the primitive tools found in the same strata. In 1960, one of Dr Leakey's sons, Jonathan, found the skull and bones of a ten-year-old child, and in 1962 another skull having the same characteristics as the child was found. These bones belonged to a species called by Leakey *Homo habilis*, a primitive

4   The Evolution of Man

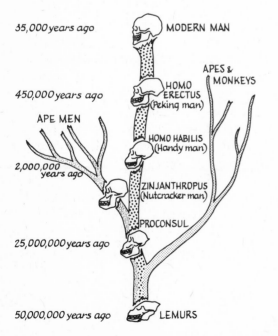

5   The Great Rift Valley

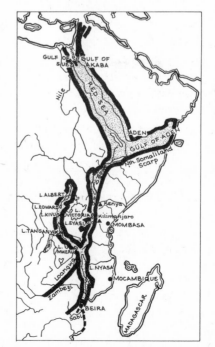

man with lighter bones than *Zinjanthropus*, a larger brain and more dexterous fingers. Both these types lived at the same time, and it is generally thought that *Zinjanthropus* developed into the various types of ape-men that have been found in South Africa and elsewhere, while *Homo habilis* was the remote ancestor of modern man.

About ten thousand years ago the large stone tool called a 'hand-axe' (but really a combination hammer, chopper and scraping tool) was superseded by a host of smaller and better-made tools. Knives, spears, needles and scrapers tell us of man's increasing ability to use his hands. He not only hunted for food, but made clothes from the skins and ornaments from the bones of the animals he killed. From these tools he advanced to the working of obsidian, which is a black volcanic rock that can be chipped into flakes and made into extremely sharp knives, arrow heads and barbs for fishing spears.

By about 4000 B.C. there were three quite distinct races inhabiting the continent of Africa. The direct descendant of *Homo habilis* lived on the open plains that covered most of East Africa. He was a hunter who preyed on the abundant game and resembled the present-day Bushman who lives in the Kalahari Desert. He made no permanent settlements but followed the game as it roamed over the plains, making a temporary encampment until the herds moved on.

To the north in the great fertile valley of the Nile there grew up a race of farmers and cattle keepers who originated in south-west Asia and spread into the Nile from the river civilisations of the Euphrates and Tigris. These people are called Hamites and they are distinguished by a very fine bone structure and light-coloured skins. They developed rapidly in the kindly environment of the Nile and pushed southwards through what is now Ethiopia, the Sudan and Uganda, driving the Bushman from the attractive savannah lands and confining him to the inhospitable deserts and the dense mountain forests.

A completely different race, whose origin is still a mystery, was developing along the Congo River and its tributaries. These people had very large bones which were, however, light in density, and a jet black skin. They are therefore physically distinct from the Hamites and are, in fact, the ancestors of the modern Negro or Bantu tribes. The relative ease of life in the Congo Basin enabled them to multiply quicker than their neighbours on the open plains and they, in their turn, pushed eastwards and southwards so that by the first century B.C. the primitive Bushman had been almost completely driven out of East Africa by the twin thrusts of the Hamites from the north and the Bantu from the west.

The Bantu invaders brought with them civilisation and stability of organisation. From the Red Sea to the Senegal River and southwards, Africa became covered with 'Kingdoms' all remarkably similar and obviously deriving their social structure from a common source. The king was a divine or semi-divine personage. His health was of paramount importance to his subjects, for upon it depended the crops, the animals, the fertility of the land and the coming of the rains. The king was therefore shut away in complete seclusion, usually in a 'royal' town that was devoted solely to his comfort. When he fell ill or became old he was ritually killed and entombed, often with the offering of human sacrifice. Under the king were a host of officials whose main purpose was to raise the necessary tributes of food and labour to support the king and the inhabitants of the royal township. In most of these kingdoms all external trade was a royal monopoly and the export of ivory, hides, gold, copper

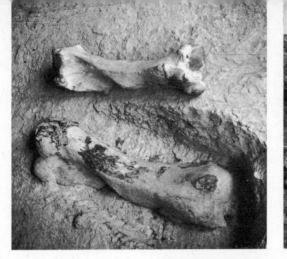

6 & 7   Ologersailie, in the Rift Valley south of Nairobi, is the site of
a Stone Age 'factory' where tools and weapons were manufactured.
*Left*, the leg-bone of an elephant that lived at that time compared
with a modern one. *Right*, 'hand axes' in various stages of
completion; the round stone is part of a bolas. Three such stones
were connected to thongs of hide and thrown around the feet of
game animals, tripping them up so that they could be clubbed

and precious stones was controlled by the king. This strong centralised government based
on a farming economy contrasted with the rather loose family structure of the primitive
hunters and the Hamitic cattle raisers, whose nomadic existence made any strong form of
government impossible.

At the same time as the great inland kingdoms were being established the coast of
Africa was being explored and exploited by traders from Arabia. The monsoon winds
blowing regularly in one direction for months at a time made the southward exploration of
the continent relatively easy for these early navigators.

The pattern of sailing and of the boats used in these seas has changed little over the last
two thousand years. With the onset of the north-easterly monsoon in December the dhows
and bagallas come flocking down from the Persian Gulf, their great sails driving them before
the wind. By April, when the south-easterly monsoon is established, they have completed
their trading and are ready to start on the return journey, running once more before the
wind.

From the first century A.D. comes the first written account of life in the area. It is contained in a book called *The Periplus of the Erythrean Sea*, written by a Greek trader of the
Roman Empire living in Egypt. The name 'Erythrean Sea' was given to all the water that
extended eastwards from Africa; 'Periplus' means a guide. The book tells of the series of
settlements established down the coast, which was called at that time Azania. The traders
brought iron goods and glass, specially manufactured for the trade, together with wine and
wheat as gifts. They took back with them ivory, rhinoceros horn, tortoise shell, cinnamon,
palm oil and slaves. Some Arabs stayed and took local wives. The outcome of this inter-
marrying was the emergence of a separate group called Swahili, from the Arabic meaning
'Coast people', and the establishment of an Arabic culture along the whole of the Coast.
With the coming of Islam the Arabs of the Oman and Muscat converted the coastal Swahili

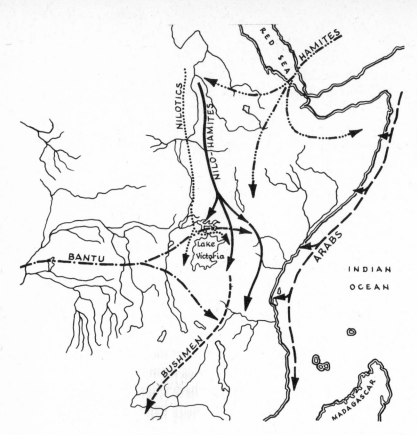

8 The movements of the various races into East Africa. The twin thrusts of the Bantu and the Nilo-Hamites drove the primitive Bushmen from the open plains into the inhospitable forests and deserts

to the new religion and this acted as a link between the two areas as strong as the ties of blood. By the thirteenth century the whole of the trade of the Indian Ocean was in the hands of the Arabs. They spread across the sea to India, Malaya, Java, and Sumatra, taking their religion with them and converting the peoples they met in these areas to Islam.

There are many ruins on the Coast of East Africa that date from this period. From the excavations which have been made, particularly at Gedi in Kenya and on the Island of Kilwa off the coast of Tanzania, we can build up a very good picture of the life of the coastal towns. The merchants lived in spacious houses, with walls built of coral, plastered and painted. The roofs were flat and made of lime plaster carried on beams of mangrove poles. Many of the houses had interior courtyards and some had special bathing places fed by running water. There was a large palace for the ruler of the city, with public rooms for the dispensing of justice, strong rooms for the storage of trade goods and special quarters for the women. The largest and best building was nearly always the mosque. This had a semi-circular apse (called the *qibla*) in the centre of the north wall to show the direction of Mecca, with a pulpit to the right. The mosque roof was often vaulted and tiled instead of being flat but there was very seldom a minaret, for the Arabs of the Oman belonged to a strict Islamic sect that forbade such embellishments.

In addition to the trade with Arabia there must at this time have been quite an extensive trade with China. Plates, bowls and dishes of Chinese porcelain have been found in abundance at the coastal sites. Some particularly fine pieces were let into the pillars of tombs, most probably as a sign of the wealth or standing of the buried person, and many of these pillars complete with bowls still remain. The Chinese did not, however, trade directly with the East African coast. They traded with the Arabs in India and the Far East and the Arabs brought their goods on to Azania where they were used to buy slaves and the African ivory which was particularly highly prized in China. There is a record of a live giraffe being sent as a present to the Emperor of China in 1414, and at least once (in 1418) an expedition from China actually reached Malindi, but it carried back a most depressing picture of the continent. Cheng Ho, the leader of the expedition, reported that 'the people were black, their nature fierce, they are the worst of barbarians'.

So prosperous did this coast become that primitive barter was replaced by money trade. Chinese copper coins have been found dating back to A.D. 713 at Kilwa, which also minted its own copper coinage, recognised throughout the area. Arab sailors brought benefits of another kind, for it is during this period that they introduced to Africa the coconut palm, the banana and the tapioca plant from the East Indies and oranges from China.

The centuries-long grip of the Arabs on the East African Coast was broken at last by the sudden arrival of the Portuguese. They had been searching for a long time for a sea route to the Indies, as the land route to these riches was blocked by the Muslim forces that held the arc of countries from the Danube to the Nile. With dogged persistence the Portuguese Navigators had pushed slowly farther and farther down the West Coast of Africa battling against ocean currents, head winds, sickness and hostile tribes. This outflanking movement was the dream of Prince Henry but it took nearly eighty years to explore the West Coast. But once Bartholomew Diaz had rounded the Cape of Good Hope in 1486 it was only twelve years before Vasco da Gama arrived off the coast of East Africa.

On his first voyage Vasco da Gama called at Mombasa and Malindi where he built a large pillar that stands to this day. On his second voyage he called at Sofala and learnt of the gold mines of the interior; he also learnt that the gold trade was controlled by the Sultan of Kilwa. Vasco da Gama immediately sailed for Kilwa with a safe conduct given him by the Governor. In spite of the fact that the safe conduct said that he came in peace, he treacherously captured the Sultan's deputy, an Arab called Amir Muhammed Kiwahi. For this hostage he then extorted a ransom of gold from the Amir and a promise that he would acknowledge the King of Portugal as his sovereign.

During the next few years there were several smaller voyages from Portugal but it was in 1505 that the main force set out to capture the towns along the trade route to the Indies. The Leader of the Expedition was Francisco d'Almeida and he left Lisbon with twenty ships and over 1,500 men. He captured Sofala and Kilwa, where he left a garrison of about 120 men, sacked and burnt Mombasa, then continued on his journey to India.

By 1509 the Portuguese had completed their domination of the Coast. They made no attempt at colonisation. They were interested only in the trade with India and the spice islands; apart from the gold from Sofala their interest in East Africa was solely as a staging post for their fleets. Soon, however, the Navigators found that the best route to India was to strike across the Ocean from Mozambique using the monsoon wind rather than hugging the Coast to Malindi. So although the Portuguese remained in nominal control of the Coast, they held it without any large commitment of men or arms.

In 1585 a Turkish pirate named Mirale Bey sailed down the Coast from the Red Sea, exhorting the Swahili to throw off the Portuguese domination. Mombasa agreed to join Mirale Bey but Malindi remained loyal to Portugal and called for help to Goa (the Portuguese colony in India). A Portuguese fleet arrived in 1587 and recaptured Mombasa, but Mirale Bey re-occupied it as soon as the fleet sailed back to Goa, and set about preparing an invasion of Malindi. A strange horde now appeared on the scene, composed of a cannibal tribe called the Zimba, who had trekked from their home on the Zambesi River, killing, destroying and eating everything that lay in their path. They razed Kilwa in 1587, then worked their way up the Coast until they appeared before Mombasa in 1589, just as the Portuguese attacked the ships of Mirale Bey and drove him back into the town. The Zimba offered their help to the Portuguese, who were at first reluctant to ally themselves to the cannibals. When they did accept their help, the Zimba stormed Mombasa and massacred the inhabitants.

The Zimba then struck north to Malindi and launched an all-out attack against the town. A handful of Portuguese, who made up the garrison of Malindi, fought desperately with their old allies, the Arabs, against the Zimba, but the walls were breached and the Zimba were actually pouring into the town when they were taken in the rear by the Wasegeju – a tribe who had been friendly with Malindi for many years. The Wasegeju completely destroyed the Zimba and saved Malindi from the fate of Mombasa. In 1593, as a result of these battles, the Portuguese decided to establish greater control over the Coast and began building a stronghold, which they called Fort Jesus, on the island of Mombasa.

The Fort was built at the entrance to the harbour on a high ridge of coral. It is very cleverly sited at the point where ships are forced close into the shore by the shoals and currents of the channel. The coral was cut back to a vertical face below the walls of the Fort, which are over fourteen feet thick. The architect of Fort Jesus was an Italian, João Batista Cariato, who worked for the Portuguese as their Chief Architect of India. The design of the fort was his last work. He poured into it all the knowledge he had acquired during the years he had worked in the East and he made it immensely strong. Every wall was covered by a projecting bastion so that attackers were constantly under fire, whilst on the seaward side there was a projecting gun platform with the walls of the flanking bastions swept backwards to increase the field of fire for the guns. The landward side of the Fort was defended by a deep ditch with an overhanging lip which provided shelter for the townspeople during attacks from the sea. Fort Jesus was impregnable to the usual methods of siege, as the solid coral on which it stood made mining under the walls impossible, whilst scaling the walls would have been extremely costly in lives due to the enfilading fire from the bastions. It changed hands several times in the next three hundred years, but usually as a result of starvation or sickness of the garrison. Only once, when it was bombarded by rockets and shells in 1875 by the British men-of-war *Nassau* and *Riflemen*, was it surrendered by the occupants whilst they were still in fighting trim.

The seventeenth century was a century of continuous fighting along the East African Coast. In spite of the strength of Fort Jesus, the Portuguese hold on the Coast was never very firm. Their possessions to the north of Mozambique had become a backwater producing little and not helping the trade with the Indies. It was therefore uneconomic to

9   The gun platform of Fort Jesus, showing how it commands
the entrance channel to Mombasa Harbour

garrison them heavily. The weakness of the Portuguese was matched by the military resurgence of the Islamic states of the Persian Gulf. Arabs once more sailed down the Coast, entering into alliances with the Swahili towns and states, encouraging them to rebel against their overlords. The Arabs destroyed the Portuguese settlements in Zanzibar and Paté in 1652, and in 1669 they attacked Mozambique itself. The Portuguese made several counterattacks during the next ten years and the struggle continued fiercely until March 1696 when a large fleet from Oman attacked Fort Jesus.

At first the siege was not pressed strongly; the Arabs surrounded the Fort but were so lax in their blockade that they let one of the defenders slip through their lines to bring reinforcements. The garrison also found no difficulty in bringing supplies from the Africans on the mainland, or receiving help sent by the Queen of Zanzibar, who was their ally. By December, however, the attackers had been reinforced and they tightened their grip on the Fort, attacking twice very strongly but being repulsed. A relieving fleet arrived off the Fort on Christmas Day 1696 but it was weakly led and after landing a few reinforcements scuttled away to the flesh-pots of Mozambique. In July 1697 the defenders had been reduced by disease and starvation to the Captain of the Fort (who was in fact a civilian called Mogo de Mello), a priest and two soldiers, supported by the loyal Swahili Chief Bwana Daud with about thirty followers and forty African women. This tiny force beat off a strong attack on 20 July, a dying Portuguese soldier being carried to the swivel gun by the African women,

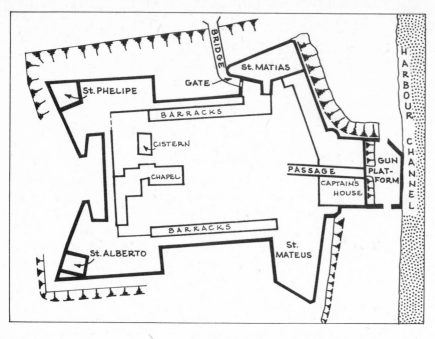

10 A plan of Fort Jesus as it was finally developed. Notice how every wall is covered by enfilading fire from the bastions at each corner so that attackers have no shelter

where he fired into the attackers whilst the women helped the men to push off the scaling ladders and hurl grenades into the mass of Arabs at the foot of the wall. Within the next week the priest and the two soldiers died, to be followed four days later by de Mello, who left Bwana Daud in charge of the Fort. He maintained the defence with unswerving loyalty, although the attackers tried to get him to join them, pointing out to him that he was a Muslim and that he should be fighting against the Portuguese, not with them. In October a relief expedition landed men and stores and the new General, Pereira de Brito, carried the offensive to the Arabs, attacking them whenever possible. In December another commander arrived to supersede de Brito. He was a disagreeable and unpopular man, who quarrelled with the loyal Swahili so that they refused to remain and were evacuated to Goa. Fort Jesus held out for another whole year, but on 13 December 1698 the Arabs heard that the total garrison was reduced to eight Portuguese, three Indians and two African women. They attacked at night and after bitter fighting by the survivors captured the Fort. The Captain died charging the Arabs, firing his blunderbuss. Two of the other Portuguese lured a large number of Arabs into the Powder Magazine by telling them it contained a hoard of gold. When they crowded inside the Portuguese blew themselves up with all the Arabs.

The siege had lasted thirty-three months, had cost the Portuguese 800 of their own dead and about 3,000 Swahili. That the fort had held out so long, often with a tiny garrison, shows the natural strength of the design. There is no doubt that if Portugal had made efforts to reinforce the garrison in 1698 as in the previous years, Fort Jesus would never have fallen. As it was, the capture of the Fort signalled the final disintegration of the Portuguese hold on the Coast. The old pattern of Swahili city states, governed by Arab dynasties from the Oman, was soon re-established and the links with the Islamic culture and trade of the Persian Gulf once more set the pattern of life on the East African Coast.

# 2 History 1700-1880

FIGHTING CONTINUED during the early years of the eighteenth century. From 1700 to 1740 the Omani Arabs were trying to impose their rule on the towns that had rid themselves of the Portuguese. The towns, not surprisingly, were very reluctant to give up their hard-won freedom and exchange their Portuguese overlords for Omanis. By 1740, however, Oman had re-established her hold on the Coast and there were Omani Governors and garrisons in all the important towns. Naturally the Governors were of the ruling dynasty of Oman, the Mazrui. When this family was overthrown by the rival Busaidi clan in 1741, and Ahmedbin Said el-Busaidi seized the Sultanate of Oman, the Mazrui Governors of East Africa refused to recognise the new régime. They severed connections with Oman and declared themselves independent. The rulers in Oman then had the task of once more subjugating the Coast. The struggle continued for over a century and led, indirectly, to the rise of Zanzibar. For here the ruling family were members of the El-Harthi clan who remained staunchly loyal to the Busaidi dynasty, providing a firm base for the Omani forces, and growing rich and powerful in the process.

The century also saw the growth of the slave trade. There had, of course, been a trade in slaves from the earliest times, but the demand was not great, as the only use for slaves was as household labour. This was changed in 1735 when La Bourdonnais was appointed governor of the Île de France (Mauritius). He was a ruthless and ambitious man, determined to make his island fruitful and productive. He extended the sugar plantations, introduced cotton and built factories, roads and bridges. All this development needed a huge labour force which could only be obtained by buying slaves.

At first this demand for slaves was met by supplies from Madagascar. When these dried up, La Bourdonnais turned to Zanzibar and Kilwa, the nearest points on the Coast. In 1776 a Frenchman named Morice obtained a concession for an exclusive trade in slaves from the Sultan's dominions and from this time onwards the French became the main European slave traders along the East African Coast, though Dutch, Portuguese and Americans were also engaged in the area. The growth of the American and West Indian plantations with their need for labour led to an exactly similar increase in the slave trade on the West Coast of Africa where the trade became concentrated in British, German and American hands.

By the end of the eighteenth century there was considerable agitation in England for the abolition of the slave trade. This was matched by the feeling in France, where the Revolution, with its ideals of Liberty, Equality and Fraternity, caused many to reconsider their views on the rightness of slavery. This liberality of thought was not apparent in the colonies of the two countries or in America, where the economic pressure for cheap and plentiful labour over-ruled humanitarian sentiments. It was not until 1807 after thirty years of

11  The fort at Kilwa built, like Fort Jesus, to command the anchorage. Note the massive construction of the outside walls

constant agitation that Britain prohibited slavery, but once having done this, she attacked it with great thoroughness along the West Coast. This attack was all the more commendable as it was carried out at a time when Britain's resources were severely strained in fighting the Napoleonic Wars. In East African waters the effort was not so prompt, for not only was the scene of action very much farther away but also Britain had concluded a treaty with the Sultan of Oman. By this treaty the Sultan agreed to help Britain to keep the French out of the Indian Ocean. Britain was careful, therefore, not to antagonise the Sultan by stopping the main trade of his dominions. A further twist was given to the situation when Britain captured the Île de France in 1810 and took over a slave-based economy, which she was forced, for economic reasons, to support.

The actual collection of slaves on the mainland was always in Arab hands. In the early days slavery had been a by-product of the ivory trade. Caravans of Arabs had marched into the interior to hunt ivory which was always in great demand. When they had shot a sufficient amount they captured local Africans and forced them to act as porters to carry the tusks to the Coast. Once they had arrived there, the Africans were sold either to other traders or to plantation owners. As the demand grew, raiding parties were sent out to trade for slaves. Fortified staging posts were set up along the main slave routes. Warlike tribes such as the Yao in the south, the Wanyamwezi and the Baganda round the lakes, were encouraged to prey upon their weaker neighbours and sell the captives to the Arabs who supplied guns, gunpowder and ammunition in exchange.

Once captured, the slave was manacled to the next man and his neck imprisoned in a forked stick, the stem of which rested on the shoulder of the man in front during the march. The slaves were then driven 500 to 600 miles to the Coast, carrying ivory or other trade goods on their heads. Women and children were captured as well as men and made to carry a burden. Any who grew weak or ill were killed immediately and left to rot by the side of the path. Livingstone describes one column he saw that was composed of 500 slaves; their necks

18

chafed and bleeding with their bonds, being beaten along the path at a jog trot, tears streaming from their eyes. The slave paths converged until they became great roads to the Coast. Two of these ended at Kilwa and Lindi, but the largest ended at a town just opposite Zanzibar. A town which still bears the name it was given by the slaves as they passed through it to embark and leave their country for ever – Bagamoyo – 'throw away your heart'.

At the Coast the slaves were packed into dhows. The bottom layer was arranged so that they were standing shoulder to shoulder, with no room to move. When this layer was complete, a temporary deck was laid on beams a few inches over their heads, and on this another layer was packed in and so on. Often the crossing to Zanzibar took several days, during which time the slaves were left without food or water. At the height of the trade at the end of the eighteenth century, 15,000–20,000 slaves were passing through Zanzibar slave market in a year. These represented the survivors of a mortality rate of seventy-five per cent of the slaves originally captured. It has been estimated that over 10 million Africans were captured by slavers in East Africa. Traders who knew the interior well told Sir John Kirk that where there used to be a village every two or three miles, they now went for days with nobody in sight. Behind Lindi and Kilwa the land was completely depopulated for eighteen days' march inland.

On their arrival at Zanzibar the slaves were unloaded from the dhows and paraded through the town, the best specimens at the head of the procession where the owner walked, crying the good points of his wares. The actual market was held in the cool of the evening, after which the slaves were either taken to their new masters' plantations in Zanzibar, these being the lucky ones; or, more probably, driven to one of the slave pens on the beaches to await onward shipment to Mauritius, Arabia or the East Indies. A journey entailing hardship, sickness and horror that cannot now be conceived.

Side by side with the slave trade there grew up a legitimate trading network that used the same paths and tracks, often the same caravans. By the middle of the nineteenth century nearly every large inland settlement had at least one Arab or Indian trader in residence and in constant contact with Zanzibar. These traders imported their own civilisation – they taught the local Africans to build rectangular houses with doors instead of the traditional round hut and to cultivate new crops. They also brought new trees – coconuts, casuarina, bougainvillea and date palm, so that wherever they settled they created a small oasis in the bush. Nowadays, as one journeys across what looks like virgin bushland, one often comes across a grove of three or four huge mango trees, their deep green leaves providing a welcome shade from the heat. These great trees are all that are left of some Arab encampment or trading post, the only reminders of an empire that has vanished.

In 1805 Seyyid Said bin Sultan seized the throne of Oman by stabbing the ruler. So came to power a man who was to play a decisive part in East African affairs for the next half-century. He inherited the treaty of aid and friendship which had been signed between Oman and Britain in 1798, and until 1815 this treaty ensured that very little pressure was brought to bear on him regarding the slave trade within his dominions. The defeat of Napoleon freed naval ships from European waters and a squadron sailed for the Persian Gulf, its first priority the suppression of piracy in these seas. The hunting down of the pirates who infested the Gulf by the ships of the Royal Navy cemented the friendship between the two countries, for it allowed Oman to trade very much more freely with their East African dependencies. This increasing friendship still left the dilemma of slavery, for if all slave trading were to be abolished, Said's subjects would certainly revolt against him, while to condone the trade was morally impossible for Britain. After much negotiation a compromise treaty, called the Moresby Treaty after the British negotiator, was signed in 1822. This prohibited the export or sale of slaves by Oman to the subjects of any Christian power and gave to the Royal Navy the power to seize any Arab ships violating the decree. The treaty defined the area under the suzerainty of Oman; within this area slave trading between Muslims was allowed. Enforcement of the treaty was almost impossible in the vastness of the Indian Ocean. Every Arab trader was intent on breaking the law and, in addition to the difficulty of actually catching the slave ships, there was the impossibility of deciding if the slaves in transit along the East African seaboard were consigned to a Muslim or a Christian destination.

The treaty had another effect, for in defining the area it gave Said a title to a huge territory over which his actual control was minimal. Zanzibar he held firmly, but many of the coastal towns still had very deep loyalties to the Mazrui and some were openly hostile to the Busaidi. This was amply demonstrated in the next year. Captain William Fitzwilliam Wentworth Owen was engaged in surveying the East African Coast. A Welshman, he had a loathing for the slave trade and all who took any part in it. He was a superb hydrographer and his work is still the basis of the Admiralty Charts of East Africa. While calling for stores at Bombay in 1823, he was told that the Mazrui Governor of Mombasa was disaffected and wished to secede from Oman. Owen called on Said on his way back to East Africa and told him that he would take over Mombasa if asked, for he did not consider that Said was

12   A photograph of the slave market in Zanzibar taken by Grant in 1875 with his own annotations. Apart from the historic value of this photograph, it is of interest also as having been taken with a stereoscopic camera; the two images fuse into a three-dimensional picture

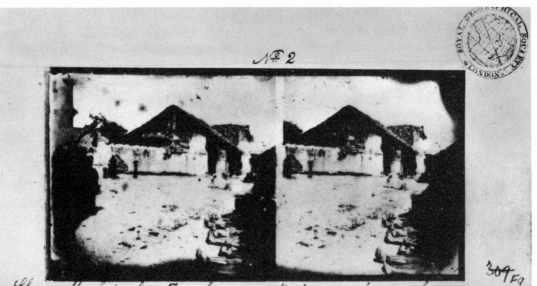

enforcing the terms of the Moresby Treaty. Said treated Owen most courteously during his stay, but immediately he left protested most strongly to Bombay at what he considered a gross intrusion into the domestic politics of his Sultanate. Meanwhile Owen had arrived at Mombasa and received it on behalf of the British Government from its local Governor. He embarked a force of local troops and tried to regain Pemba for Mombasa, but was met by an absolute refusal. He then left Lieutenant John Reitz (who was twenty-one years old), a midshipman, a corporal of marines and three seamen to hold Mombasa and continued on his way to Zanzibar, where, not surprisingly, he received a very cool welcome. This action of Owen's, made completely on his own initiative, caused years of diplomatic wrangling: Seyyid Said emphasised the recognition accorded him in the Moresby Treaty, while the Governor of Bombay, Mountstuart Elphinstone, tried to weigh the advantages of friendship and co-operation with Said against the obvious weakness of his claim to Mombasa and the very tenuous hold he had on it. By 1826 the Protectorate established in Mombasa was proving to be very unpopular. There were constant complaints about the imposition of customs dues and trading restrictions. Britain therefore decided to disallow Owen's action, and evacuated the remainder of the garrison in H.M.S. *Helicon*. Thus ended the first of the British East African Protectorates.

As soon as the news of the departure of the British reached Said, he organised a fleet and sailed with it to Mombasa to recapture the town from the Mazrui. He arrived off Fort Jesus in 1828, when, after a bombardment of the town and some parleying, the Fort and town capitulated. He left a strong garrison to hold the area and sailed on to Zanzibar, which he had not visited before. The contrast between the arid deserts of Oman and the green lushness of Zanzibar at once captivated him. He decided to make Zanzibar his capital, a decision that had far-reaching effects on East Africa, for it focused within the area the seat of government and the centre of trade. It ensured that the island became the most important place in East Africa for the rest of the century.

Very slowly the fight against the slave trade went on. In 1840, in return for British help against the French who were trying to annex a small island off Madagascar called Nossi Bé, Seyyid Said agreed to forbid the export of slaves from Africa to Arabia. The difficulty of implementing this agreement, particularly as the slave market in Zanzibar was not closed down, made it virtually ineffectual. Little was done until 1856, when Seyyid Said died leaving seventy wives and 112 children. He was succeeded by his son, Seyyid Majid, a weak and timid man who became shifty and dissolute as he grew older. In 1858 C. P. Rigby was appointed British Consul in Zanzibar. A man of fierce and sudden temper, he was a lifelong hater of slavery, the results of which he had met often in Arabia before being posted to East Africa. He found an appalling situation on his arrival, for during the latter part of Said's reign the British Consul Hammerton had done little to enforce the treaties, as he had developed a strong friendship for the Sultan and did not feel he could coerce him too strongly. Dead and dying slaves lay on the beaches and in the town. Every day files of emaciated slaves were driven through the streets from dhows to the slave pens.

Rigby pressed constantly for naval reinforcements, as the forces at his disposal were completely inadequate for the task. In order to cover as much of the area as possible the warships had to dispatch small parties in open boats to hunt slave dhows individually. The difficulties and dangers of this method cannot be over-stressed. The boats were tiny, loaded to the gunwales with stores and arms; the crews exposed to the tropical sun day after day with inadequate provisions and virtually no medicines; the sea shark-infested and much of the land a malarial mangrove swamp. Despite this the Navy kept up a steady pressure on the slavers. In the last years of Rigby's Consulship, two old warships, the *Lyra* and the *Gorgon*, between them captured sixty dhows. They came to be treated with a superstitious hatred by the Arab dhow captains and H.M.S. *Lyra* was known to them as '*El Shaitan*' – the devil.

Rigby realised that the real attack on slavery should be made on land, and he took every opportunity he could of pursuing this policy. He carried out many raids on slave-owning Indians on the island, for as they were British subjects he could enforce the decree against slave-owning on them. He used to haul offenders through the streets in chains to judgement. His crusade required great personal courage, for there were several attempts on his life, but by the time he left he had personally emancipated over 8,000 slaves.

Majid was succeeded in 1870 by his brother, Bargash, an energetic ruler who had a passionate interest in trade, the acquisition of wealth and the leading of a life of luxury. The Consul, Dr (later Sir John) Kirk, was a man of great determination who was deeply under the spell of Livingstone. He obtained great influence over Bargash and in 1873 persuaded him (helped it is true by the presence of several British warships in the harbour) to issue an edict totally prohibiting the export of slaves from any part of his dominions. When slavers tried to get round this by marching their slaves along the Coast Bargash was persuaded to raise a force of troops under the command of a naval lieutenant, Lloyd William Matthews, who had been engaged in anti-slavery operations on the Coast for two years. Matthews had a deep identification with the Arabs and gave to Bargash and his successor a lifetime of devoted and loyal service. Starting with the command of the small force of troops, he ended as Chief Minister to Bargash. Between them Kirk and Matthews completed the work of stamping out the slave trade in East Africa, the market in Zanzibar was finally closed and a great cathedral was built on the site.

At the same time as the fight against slavery along the Coast was proceeding, there was a mounting tide of exploration that crumbled the barrier of ignorance that for long had hidden the interior of the 'dark continent'. At the beginning of the nineteenth century the Coast was well known, but knowledge of the interior is summed up in Swift's verse –

'So Geographers in Afric maps,
With savage pictures fill their gaps
And o'er uninhabitable downs,
Place elephants for want of towns.'

Since earliest times there had been a tradition of great lakes and 'Mountains of the Moon' inland. The first mention of them is from a journey that a Greek trader called Diogenes claimed to have made a few centuries B.C. The original text is lost but Ptolemy in A.D. 150 quotes the account of how Diogenes 'landed at Rhaptum, journeyed inland for twenty-five days, and arrived in the vicinity of the two great lakes and the snowy range of mountains whence the Nile draws its twin sources.' The legend of the great snowy peaks and the Nile source is also mentioned by Herodotus, who called the peaks Crophi and Mophi. However, when the first news of the interior of East Africa was sent to England, mentioning the existence of a large snowy mountain, it was flatly disbelieved, despite the long geographical tradition and the fact that the explorer was a missionary and therefore presumably truthful.

Ludwig Krapf was born in Germany in 1810. When he was eleven years old he was severely beaten for something he did not do and was seriously ill for six months. During this time he said he 'thought much and dwelt much on eternity'. The result of this illness and introspection was a strong vocation to Christianity, so when he was old enough he joined the Church Missionary Society in England. After working in Ethiopia for some years he arrived at Zanzibar in 1844. Seyyid Said, who grew very fond of him, helped him to settle in Mombasa to start a mission station. Here his wife and baby daughter died of malaria within a few weeks of landing so he threw himself into the work of learning the language and finding a suitable permanent site for the mission. Such was his application that within five months he had produced a translation of the New Testament into Swahili. In 1846 he was joined at Rabai, where he had founded the mission, by Johann Rebmann. From then on the two journeyed into the interior as often as possible, though neither of them was really cut out to be an explorer. Krapf particularly seemed to be in constant trouble: his animals ran away while on safari, his gun was always either going off at the wrong time, or getting jammed, or, because he lost the ramrod, was used as a water bottle. He always carried a large umbrella, and this really appears to have been his most useful object, for he and his porters used to sleep under it at night. The umbrella also scared off a lion which was attacking the party when it was suddenly opened in the lion's face; it had exactly the same effect on a band of robbers, who fled immediately.

In 1848 Rebmann journeyed north-west from Rabai to visit the Chagga tribe. On 11 May he saw a large mountain rising from the plain with what he took to be a cloud covering the summit. His guides told him that the 'cloud' was solid and cold and after some further questions Rebmann realised that the 'cloud' must in fact be snow. He learnt that the mountain was called Kilima Njaro or 'The Shining Mountain'. In the next year Krapf, travelling north by east from Rabai towards Kitui and the Wakamba country saw the twin rock peaks of Mount Kenya with the white of snow between them. The reports of these discoveries were greeted in England with derision and disbelief. One of the chief armchair critics was W. D. Cooley, a member of the Royal Geographical Society, who wrote a long attack on the likelihood of there being such mountains, making much of Rebmann's short sight; but the perfect answer is given in Krapf's diary entry for 10 November 1849 –

'This morning we had a beautiful distant view of the snow mountain Kilimanjaro. It was high above Endara and Bura, yet even at this distance I could discern its white crown must be snow. All the arguments that Mr. Cooley has adduced against the existence of such a snow-mountain, and against the accuracy of Rebmann's report, dwindle into nothing when one has the evidence of one's own eyes of the fact before one; so that they are scarcely worth refuting.'

Krapf and Rebmann were joined by another missionary called Erhardt and all three continued their explorations, talking with Arab and Swahili traders and slave raiders and

13  John Hanning Speke (1827–64)     14  Sir Richard Burton (1821–90)

collating all the information they received. As a result they published the famous 'Slug Map' in 1856, so called because of the shape of the large lake shown in the interior. This lake combined the descriptions of Lakes Victoria, Tanganyika and Nyasa, all of which were well known to the Arabs, but which were shown as one. A mistake easily made from second-hand reports when it is realised that any large stretch of water is called 'the Sea' in Swahili and that two of the lakes lie in the Rift Valley and so have many features in common. It was the publishing of the 'Slug Map' that brought the next two explorers to Africa. Richard Burton was already a distinguished scholar, linguist and traveller; he had visited both Mecca and Medina disguised as an Arab and had collected the tales that we know as the *Arabian Nights*. He was a flamboyant character, the complete opposite of his companion John Hanning Speke, who was the son of a famous zoologist. Speke had prepared himself for exploration by making journeys into unknown parts of India collecting specimens for his father. Burton and Speke had travelled together in Somalia during 1844 and 1845, and although Speke was very scathing about Burton's habit of 'always dressing up in turban and baggy trousers' he had a high regard for his companion's abilities.

They landed at Zanzibar in 1857 and immediately visited Rebmann to talk of his journeys and discoveries. Then, after endless delays whilst their porters and animals were collected at Bagamoyo, they started into the interior. The first few days were chaotic and they averaged only about 2 to 3 miles, but gradually they settled into a routine and reached Zungomero at the foot of the Uluguru Mountains on the twenty-fourth day. Burton must

24

have still been suffering from the frustrations of the start of the journey, for he called it 'unhappy Zungomero, lead coloured above, mud coloured below, windswept, fog veiled and deluged by clouds.' Despite this the explorers stayed there for two weeks to recover before pushing on over Burton's 'Pass Terrible' to reach the 'fiery waterless plains' of Ugogo. Fever and dysentery were making them very weak so that they could hardly sit their donkeys. To this was now added the incessant delays imposed on the caravan by the chiefs through whose land they were passing and whose demands for *hongo* (tribute) became more and more outrageous. Just as they were reaching the end of their tether they fell in with an Arab caravan who helped them forward to Tabora. Here they first received the news that the lake they sought was in fact three separate lakes. This positive news cheered them immensely; excited and refreshed they travelled west until on 13 February 1858, they reached the shores of Lake Tanganyika at Ujiji. Speke was blind with sunglare and an eye infection, Burton was very ill with dysentery but they immediately set out by canoe to explore the north end of the lake, to see if the river there was in fact the Nile. After travelling some way they were bitterly disappointed to learn that the river flowed into and not out of the lake, so they returned to Tabora very crestfallen.

Relations between the two explorers now became strained as Burton wanted to pack up and go home, but Speke was determined to explore the Northern Lake. He left Burton

15   The 'Slug Map'

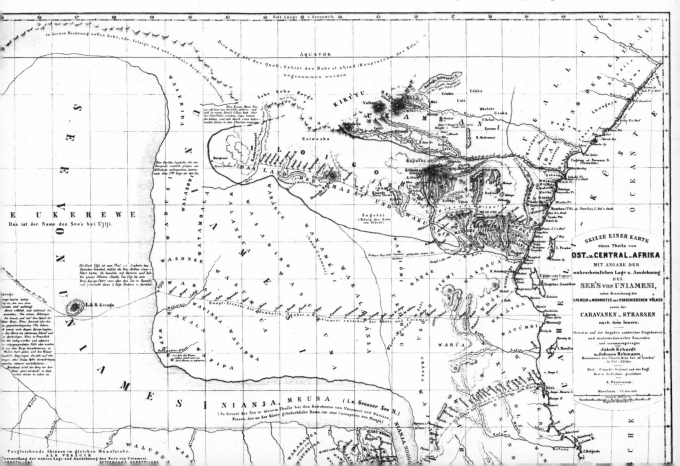

at Tabora and went on alone, reaching the southern end of the lake at the Mwanza Gulf. He followed this small inlet round until on 3 August he saw spread out before him the great shining expanse of water that stretched as far as the eye could see. He wrote in his journal, 'I no longer felt any doubt that the lake at my feet gave birth to that interesting river, the source of which has been the subject of so much speculation, and the object of so many explorers.' When Speke returned to Tabora, Burton received his news with disbelief and they journeyed back to the Coast in bitterness, with frequent quarrels.

Speke's discovery was treated with incredulity on his return to England, but he was commissioned to return to Africa by the Royal Geographical Society to try to prove his claims. He took with him this time Captain J. A. Grant, a friend from his Indian days. They left Zanzibar in October 1860, and then for three years there was no news of them. Meanwhile, whilst Speke's back was turned, Burton was mounting a vicious attack on him. Then in 1863 a telegram arrived from Speke who had reached Khartoum, 'The Nile is settled'. Speke had travelled right round the western shores of Lake Victoria, mapping as he went. He was the first European to enter Uganda and stayed with three of the great rulers: Rumanika of Karagwe, Mutesa of Buganda and Kamurasi of Bunyoro-Kitara. He remained at Mutesa's capital for several months, finding it very difficult to get away from the hospitable king, then journeyed eastwards until he struck the Nile at Bulondoganyi. He then journeyed upstream until he came to the point where the Nile left Lake Victoria, falling over a cataract that Speke named the Ripon Falls after the President of the Royal Geographical Society. Due to the presence of hostile tribes Speke did not follow the Nile all the way to Khartoum, but he struck it at several points between the Lake and Gondokoro where he met Samuel Baker who had followed it from Alexandria and was hoping to carry on to the source. Disappointed of this prize, Baker (on Speke's suggestion) explored to the north-west and discovered another large lake which he called Albert. He admitted that the river that flowed into this lake and then almost immediately out again was Speke's Victoria Nile, but misled by reports, he was convinced that Lake Albert stretched far to the south where it was fed by a large river and thus, Baker claimed, it was the true Nile source.

On Speke's return to England he was once again bitterly attacked, particularly by Burton. The tone of the attack is well illustrated by an extract from Burton's book in which he quotes a certain James M'Queen, a Fellow of the Royal Geographical Society: 'It is with disgust, that we want proper words to express, to find the first names in Europe prostituted, and especially the name of our great and gracious Sovereign insulted and degraded in giving names to places in this most barbarous and degraded country.' Livingstone, already widely respected in England, added his voice to those against Speke, for he also believed that the Nile rose far to the south and was therefore willing to discount Speke's facts in favour of his own preconceptions. The British Association arranged a debate between Speke and Burton at Bath on 16 September 1864 to see if the matter could be finalised. They met each other at noon on the 15th, then, later in the day while out shooting, Speke shot himself. Whether it was suicide or whether it was an accident will never be known, but it was a tragic and deplorable end to the life of a great explorer who had solved one of the world's oldest geographical riddles.

As a result of Speke's death, the Royal Geographical Society commissioned David

16  David Livingstone (1813–73)

17  Sir Henry Morton Stanley
    (1840–1904)

Livingstone to examine the area between Lake Nyasa and Lake Victoria to see if he could
settle the controversy. Livingstone had ten years of exploration in Africa behind him, including a crossing from east to west, the discovery of the Victoria Falls on the Zambesi and
of Lake Nyasa. All these discoveries had been made whilst he was journeying to find the site
for a great inland mission station, but this last journey was made purely for exploratory purposes. He landed at the mouth of the Ruvuma River in 1866 and pushed quickly inland to
the shores of Lake Nyasa. There was trouble from the start, desertions of his escort and
porters, acute food shortages due to the activities of the slave-raiders, and constant thefts –
including a most valuable box of medical stores. He reached Lake Tanganyika in 1867 and
had to rest for over a month as he was seriously ill. Then for the next two years he explored
to the west of the lake, trying to sort out whether the rivers and lakes he discovered belonged
to the Nile or Congo systems, for he was still convinced that the Nile rose to the south of
Lake Victoria.

Livingstone reached Ujiji in March 1869, where he was met with the news that the
stores that he had arranged to be sent from Zanzibar to wait for him had been looted. He
rested for a while in Ujiji and then once more crossed to the west of the lake and for the next
two years carried on his explorations of the Manyema country. He became extremely weak
from fever and dysentery and, at the same time, found that the depredations of the slave
traders in this area were turning the Africans against him. His diaries at this time are full of
descriptions of the horrors of the slave trade the result of which he saw all around him. In
October 1871 he crossed back to Ujiji to find, once more, that the stores consigned to him
by Kirk from Zanzibar had all been stolen. Only a few days later help came to him out of
the blue with the arrival of Henry Morton Stanley with his historic salutation, 'Dr Livingstone, I presume?'

Stanley had been sent by the *New York Herald* to find Livingstone, who had been 'lost' for five years. He brought with him a wealth of stores, but even more important he gave Livingstone the human contact he needed. Together they explored the lake to the north and travelled back to Tabora, where they lived together for two months before Stanley had to start back to the Coast from where he arranged for further stores to be sent to Ujiji. When Livingstone received them, he turned south, determined to solve to his satisfaction the problem of the Congo/Nile watershed. He gradually became weaker and weaker, having to be carried on a litter wherever he went. On 17 April 1873 he arrived at Chitambo's village near Lake Bangweulu and made his last diary entry that he was 'knocked up quite'. Here he remained, too weak to move. On the morning of 1 May his servants found him dead, kneeling by the side of his bed. They preserved the body as well as they could and then carried it, with all Livingstone's papers, to Bagamoyo. The supreme loyalty and devotion of this act can only be appreciated when it is remembered that a dead body was a powerful taboo and usually a thing of the most dreadful ill-omen to the African; to carry one nearly 600 miles was an unexampled gesture of affection and respect.

The death of Livingstone was the end of the classic period of African exploration. A great deal of exploration was done in the next years by missionaries, for the journey of Livingstone's body to the Coast and thence to burial in Westminster Abbey gave a great impetus to missionary effort in Africa. Stanley, whose writings were responsible for much of this increase in missionary effort, was also the instrument for the new phase in the exploration of the continent. His great journeys opened up the country, but his constant flow of dispatches focused the eyes of the world on Africa, brought its vast potential to the notice of Europe and started the international scramble for power in Africa.

18   The historic meeting at Ujiji. A print from Stanley's account of his search *How I found Livingstone*

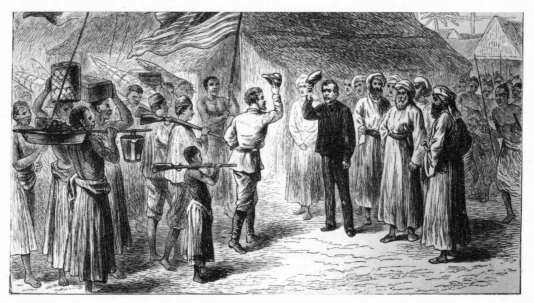

# 3 History 1880 to the present

THE MOVES AND COUNTERMOVES, the machinations and treacheries of the scramble for Africa have the complexities of a game of six-handed chess and make an absorbing study in themselves. In East Africa there were only two powers involved to any great extent, though King Leopold's free-booting activities in the Congo also had repercussions in the area. Even with only the two powers, it is necessary to go behind the apparent facts and understand the real motives of the Governments concerned. Britain had to keep Germany's friendship, for Germany supported her *de facto* annexation of Egypt in 1882. Germany was also willing to support France in Africa in order to divert from herself French hatred for the loss of Alsace and Lorraine during the Franco-Prussian War. Britain did not really want to enter the scramble for colonies in Africa for she had her hands full of trouble both in South Africa and in Egypt and the Sudan, but was forced to compete for strategic reasons and also in order to have a position to bargain from. Germany, very belatedly, was on the hunt for colonies in order to satisfy the urge of her people to emigrate from Europe and to ensure that such émigrés had a German Empire to go to rather than settling in the United States, Australia or South Africa, as they had been doing and so becoming lost to the Fatherland.

The stirrings of German colonialism were brought to a head in East Africa by the arrival of Carl Peters in Zanzibar in 1884. Peters was a young idealist who had been a founder member of the Society for German Colonisation. He was ruthless, rash, impatient and completely unprincipled, with a consuming desire to extend Germany's colonial empire. Zanzibar was not actually under a British Protectorate at this time, but her power in the island was almost absolute and Peters had to come to the island masquerading as a mechanic. After fitting himself out he crossed with his two companions Count Pfeil and Dr Juhlke to the mainland and travelled up the Wami River collecting treaties from every chief and sub-chief he could trick into signing. It is quite impossible for the chiefs to have had the remotest idea of what they were doing or signing but to the outside world the spurious treaties seemed very effective proof of 'occupation'. Peters rushed to Berlin with his scraps of paper, founded the German East Africa Company, transferred the treaties to it and persuaded Bismarck to declare the area a German Protectorate.

The Sultan of Zanzibar protested strongly to Britain about the declaration, pointing out that it was over his territory. In this protest he was backed by Sir John Kirk. Protests also came from the newly formed British East Africa Company who had valid commercial treaties with chiefs in the Kilimanjaro and Voi areas obtained with the sanction of the Sultan. These protests were unavailing for not only did Britain have to acquiesce in the German actions, she was also losing interest in Zanzibar. It had been the suppression of the slave trade that brought her to Zanzibar, and now that all had been done that could be done from there, Britain was not going to put herself out for the sake of the Sultan. Disappointed

19  Zanzibar in 1875, showing the great concentration of shipping.
To the right in the panorama is the Sultan's palace

by the lack of support the Sultan decided to act by himself. He refused to recognise the
German Protectorate and sent his own troops under General Matthews to re-establish his
authority in the Kilimanjaro area. Matthews travelled to the mountain and at a large meeting
of chiefs, led by Mandara of the Chagga tribe, he obtained a re-affirmation of their continuing loyalty to the Sultan and a firm promise that they would resist any attempts to sway
them from this new pact. No sooner had Matthews turned for the Coast than Juhlke arrived,
made a bond of blood-brotherhood between himself and Mandara and obtained a treaty
from him ceding all his lands and his sovereignty to the German East Africa Company.

In August 1885 a large squadron of German warships dropped anchor off Zanzibar
and Commodore Päschen presented to the Sultan a document setting out the Sultan's
agreement to the German protectorates already established. The demand was presented
while all the warships were ostentatiously clearing their decks for action and Seyyid Bargash
had no alternative but to agree, though he made it plain in the treaty that he did so 'in con-
sequence of the demand which comes to us from His Majesty the Emperor of Germany as
an Ultimatum'. The Admiral of the squadron then arrived and demanded the cession of
Dar-es-Salaam, for the Germans had recognised the Sultan's sovereignty over a strip of
land ten miles from the Coast in a joint declaration, and they now needed a port in that strip
to serve their new protectorates. Once again the Sultan had to agree to this demand as by
now he knew that he would get no help from Britain. This high-handed intimidation was
carried out by the Germans at a time when they were also negotiating with Britain and
France a Commission to delimit exactly the Sultan's dominions!

The Commission duly convened, with Colonel Kitchener (as he then was) the representative of Britain. The Sultan was not represented on the Commission and despite
Kitchener's vigorous protests General Matthews was not allowed to state the Sultan's case.
The Commission travelled over the coastal portion taking evidence at all the trading centres
but so overbearing was the attitude of the German representative Schmidt there was constant friction. Schmidt finally refused to be bound by the terms of the Commission and got
in touch with Bismarck, who in turn put pressure on the British and French Governments.
Once more Britain sold out and instructions were sent to Kitchener that only the unanimous
decisions of all three Commissioners were to be reported and in cases of disagreement it was

30

the German version that was to prevail! The results of this farcical procedure were embodied in the Anglo-German Agreement of 1886 which limited the Sultan's territory to a strip ten miles wide along the Coast from Meningani Bay in the south to Kipini (at the mouth of the Tana River) in the north. The boundary between the British and German 'spheres of influence' was to be a line running from the mouth of the Umba River to the northern foothills of Kilimanjaro and thence in a straight line to the point of intersection of the parallel of latitude 1° South with the shores of Lake Victoria. The last act in this shameful affair was to obtain the assent of the Sultan to the treaty proposals. The terms were presented to him by Holmwood, the Acting British Consul, at a time when he was a very sick man. There was nothing for him to do but agree and ratify the treaty that deprived him of his dominions.

Having obtained their foothold the Germans at once started to consolidate their position with a ruthlessness and lack of consideration that very soon led to an open revolt against them. In April 1888, Seyyid Khalifa, who had succeeded his brother Bargash, signed over the ten-mile strip to the Germans for a period of fifty years and gave to them the rights to collect all customs dues. A codicil to the agreement gave the Germans the right to fly their flag alongside that of the Sultan and it was this that provided the spark that touched off the revolt. It should be remembered that there was very little communication in those days and the ordinary coastal Arab and Swahili, with generations of loyalty to Zanzibar and Islam behind him, must have been very puzzled and not a little resentful of the sudden transference of power. At Tanga, Pangani and Bagamoyo the inhabitants rioted when the Company's flag was hoisted, shots were fired, and soon a full rebellion was in progress led by a member of the El Harthi family of Zanzibar, Bushiri bin Salim. The rapidity with which the revolt spread indicates the latent hostility that there was towards the Germans. Bushiri soon had control from the Southern Highlands, where the great Hehe Chief Mkwawa joined the revolt, to the Usambaras. The British missionaries caught in these mountains were evacuated by a rescue party that was given a personal safe conduct by Bushiri. Bushiri then attacked Dar-es-Salaam unsuccessfully but forced the evacuation of Mikindani and Lindi and captured Kilwa. At this point the Imperial German Government took over control from the Company and sent out the explorer Hermann von Wissman to take charge. Wissman, with plenty of troops at his command, retook Pangani and Tanga, defeated Bushiri's forces

31

decisively twice near Bagamoyo and finally captured Bushiri himself at Kwamkoro. He was taken to Pangani and hanged on 15 December 1889.

As a result of Bushiri's rebellion the German Government took over full control of the territory and the German East Africa Company reverted to the status of a purely commercial concern. Wissman was confirmed in his appointment as Commissioner. The country was still in a very disturbed state and an immediate attempt was made to pacify the inland tribes; the war against Mkwawa, Chief of the Hehe, is described later, but there were also expeditions against the Wanyamwezi Chief Siki, the Wagogo and Chief Tagaralla of the Wajiji. For twelve years from 1891 to 1903 the Germans fought to impose their control upon the tribes and at the same time to develop the colony as quickly as possible so that it would make a useful contribution to the economy of the Fatherland. Their ruthlessness was undoubted and there was a deep resentment amongst the Africans at the various controls on their life exercised by the Germans; the levying of forced labour to develop the country's resources, the compulsory cultivation of cotton, the fact that they were now ruled by foreigners and not their own chiefs, all led to grave dissatisfaction.

For many years there had been a snake cult on a tributary of the Rufiji River. A monster that lived in the water was reputed to have given power to a few medicine men to compound a liquid that was a certain guard against evil. Many pilgrims came openly to take the medicine but by the beginning of 1905 the medicine had changed its character; it was still a potent magic, but now it provided immunity from the bullets of the Germans, turning them to water. From this the rebellion that soon erupted took its name, for '*Maji*' is the Swahili for water and the doubling of the word is a common Swahili method of emphasis, so the name might be translated as 'very watery water' or 'absolute water'. Like Bushiri's revolt the *Maji Maji* rising spread very rapidly once the original spark had been struck. The first trouble occurred at a Government cotton farm at Kibata near Kilwa manned by forced labour. In July 1905 the Arab *Akida* who ran it for the Germans fled for his life saying the workers claimed they had a medicine that would protect them against the Germans. The workers then marched to the Coast and set fire to the small town of Samanga. From this beginning the rising spread over the whole of the southern part of the country, but as soon as the element of surprise wore off the results of the rising could not be in doubt. Germany dispatched two cruisers, a company of Marines and detachments of Papuan troops from their Pacific possessions. These arrived in September 1905 and by October the counter-offensive was in full swing. The German strategy was to send columns into the affected areas to try to destroy the rebels, but they found the enemy elusive and the general populace either actively hostile or sullenly non-cooperative. It was not until 1907 that Abdulla Mpanda, one of the ringleaders of the uprising, was killed and the last resistance was crushed. The German reprisals on the Africans who had sheltered the rebels were terrible. Villages were burnt, the inhabitants butchered or carried off, crops destroyed, cows and goats slaughtered. The result was a famine that killed over 100,000 Africans. It is no wonder that it was written that the Germans created a solitude and called it Peace.

During this same period Britain had been developing her East African holdings in a very different way. With the delimitation of the spheres of influence in 1886 the British East Africa Association was granted a Royal Charter and became in 1888 the Imperial British East

20 Speke and Grant attend an audience of the Kabaka Mutesa

Africa Company with powers to administer as much of the British sphere of influence as it could obtain treaties over. The Company had already established a trading post at Machako's village 260 miles inland on the edge of the Athi Plains and traders and missionaries had reached as far as Buganda. The missionaries met with a great deal of trouble at the Court of the Kabaka, and appealed to Britain for help. Frederick Jackson, a hunter who knew the country well, was engaged by the Company in 1889 to make a reconnaissance towards the lake and the Sudanese province of Equatoria which was being held against rebels by Emin Pasha and which might prove an even richer territory than Buganda. Jackson travelled inland and at Mumia's village found letters waiting for him from Kabaka Mwanga and Charles Stopes, a trader, who had taken the lead in trying to restore the missionaries and the Kabaka to Buganda from whence they had been driven by Arab rebels and the usurper Kalema. The letters asked Jackson to come to the help of the Kabaka and the missionaries. A further letter from the C.M.S. told Jackson that the attack had been successful and the Kabaka had been restored to his throne but that help was still needed. Jackson replied that he had specific instructions not to get involved in Buganda and he journeyed northwards towards the Mount Elgon region. As soon as they heard this the Muslim rebels attacked the Kabaka once more, and a hurried letter was sent to Jackson giving him large concessions in Buganda if he would help. This letter fell into Carl Peters' hands when he arrived at Mumia's village in February 1890. He hurried to Mwanga, agreed to help him against the rebels and extracted from the Kabaka an agreement placing Buganda in the hands of the Germans. Jackson arrived at Mwanga's just after Peters had left for the Coast, having rushed there as soon as he learned that Peters had read his mail. Mwanga would not go back on his agreement with Peters despite the fact that Buganda was within the British sphere of influence, so Jackson could do nothing but set out for the Coast, taking with him two Buganda nobles to carry the news back to the Kabaka when the question of the sphere of influence was settled.

Peters' opportunism was to no avail for at the very time that he was stealing a march on Jackson, Lord Salisbury the British Prime Minister was calling a conference between the Powers in Brussels. The result of this conference was the Act of Brussels which was signed by Germany and Britain in July 1890. It ratified the boundary already established from the Coast to the shores of Lake Victoria and extended the boundary westwards along the parallel of latitude 1° South to the Congo border. The boundary between German East Africa and

33

the British possessions of Rhodesia and Nyasaland was fixed. In return for Heligoland, which was useless to Britain but of extreme strategic importance to Germany, Zanzibar, Pemba and Witu were recognised as British Protectorates.

The stabilising of the boundaries made the way clear for Britain in East Africa, but instead of seizing the chance for development the Government once again retreated from any direct involvement and left everything to the Imperial British East Africa Company. The Company was in a very difficult position as the only prospects of profitable trade lay in Buganda and the Kingdoms of the west because it was only in those areas that ivory was easily obtainable and ivory was the only commodity that had a high enough profit margin to absorb the cost of porterage to the Coast. If trade was to be increased, a railway would have to be built and the Company expected the Government to give considerable help towards the cost of the survey and the building of the line.

While the long negotiations for the financing of the railway were progressing the Company sent Captain F. D. (later Lord) Lugard to Buganda to try to make a definitive treaty with Mwanga. Lugard found the position in Buganda still very delicate, the Muslim faction was active to the west and had large forces at its command, but the rivalry and intrigue between the Catholic and Protestant parties was the real danger. In this delicate situation Lugard had great difficulty in getting Mwanga's agreement to his proposals. In return for the protection offered him by Lugard, Mwanga was to surrender his sovereignty and allow the Company to control most of his taxation and finance. The bargain was a pretty poor one from Mwanga's point of view for Lugard's party was ill disciplined and poorly armed; their ability to give much help or offer any protection was problematical. After two days of tricky negotiations Lugard enlisted the support of the Catholic chiefs and they persuaded Mwanga to agree.

In January 1891 Lugard's position was considerably strengthened by the arrival of reinforcements under Captain Williams, but his forces were still very weak and he realised that he needed a much greater military capability if he was to administer the area effectively. Such a force did exist, for when Emin Pasha abandoned Equatoria he had left behind all his Sudanese troops under Selim Bey. This army was encamped somewhere to the west and Lugard decided to try to break through to it and bring it under his control. He was spurred on in this endeavour by rumours that Emin Pasha, who was now the German Resident in Bukoba, was also trying to get his old army to join the Germans.

Between Lugard and Selim Bey lay the Muslim Baganda forces and the kingdom of Bunyoro, whose Chief Kabarega was Mwanga's enemy and would thus oppose Lugard. The British forces were not sufficient to meet the Muslims, but the Baganda rallied to their chiefs and a large army was created under the command of Apollo Kagwa the *Katikiro* (Prime Minister). This army totally defeated the Muslims, then broke up into small bands that went looting and pillaging and refused to march westward with Lugard. He decided, however, to push on with his own force and a few Batoro who had rallied to their young king Kasagama. Kabarega had deposed Kasagama and Lugard hoped to reinstate him to his kingdom so that he would have an ally in the west. During the journey Lugard negotiated a treaty of protection with the Mugabe of Ankole. He then crossed the Kazinga Channel and captured the Sultan of Katwe. He built a stockade which he called Fort George on a high spur by the lake and used it as a base for probes into the surrounding country to try to locate Selim Bey. He searched the foothills of the Ruwenzori to the south and west but found nothing. Then, when he moved north he was confronted by the main Bunyoro army under Kabarega. His troops, reinforced by a Maxim gun, were sufficient to defeat this host and he captured their whole encampment. He built another stockade called Fort Edward and reinstated Kasagama there as ruler of Toro. In return, Kasagama agreed to the same terms as the Ankole with the addition that all ivory captured in Toro was to become the property of the Company. Lugard then pushed on northwards, defeating another large Bunyoro army and finally made contact with Selim Bey at Kavalli on Lake Albert.

At first Selim Bey was unwilling to accept service with Lugard, but finally agreed and the force marched out of Kavalli over 9,000 strong, though a great number of these were women and children. These troops Lugard distributed along the route in a series of forts to protect his communications and help Kasagama to maintain his kingdom against Kabarega.

Lugard was met, on his return to Kampala, by the news that the Company was abandoning its enterprise in Buganda as the costs were proving too much for their resources – however, a donation from the C.M.S. staved off the retreat for a year and Lugard used this time to try to settle Mwanga more firmly on the throne. This done, he sailed for England to try to convince the Government of the necessity of retaining Buganda. He found a bitter campaign of criticism waiting for him, led by Captain Macdonald, the surveyor given the task of finding the railway alignment, who had arrived in Kampala only a little before Lugard left. Despite the criticism Lugard had many admirers, and in November 1892 the Government decided to send a Commissioner to Kampala to report on the situation. They chose Sir Gerald Portal, the Consul in Zanzibar, and he left for the interior with his brother, an administrator and Major Roddy Owen.

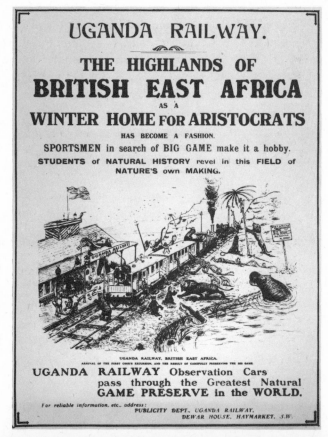

21 An early poster (c. 1900) extolling the attractions of East Africa

35

The Commissioner visited the chain of posts established by the Company at Machako's village, Fort Smith and Mumia's village and arrived at Kampala on St Patrick's Day, having taken 107 days from the Coast. He settled down to collect the facts for his report and at the same time sent his brother and Owen to withdraw the Sudanese garrisons from Toro. Owen was against this move as he realised that it would expose Kasagama but had to obey orders. Portal's brother caught a fever and returned to Kampala where he died a few days later. This loss hit the Commissioner very hard and he hurried through his final duties, leaving for the Coast two days later. He died soon after reaching England and it was two months after his death that his report was laid before Parliament. The report advocated the taking over of Buganda from the Company and the building of a railway to link Kampala to the Coast. Parliament accepted the first recommendation but not the second. After a lengthy period of negotiation with the Company as to the actual area of land to be taken over the Government declared a Protectorate over the whole of British East Africa on 1 July 1895.

The next ten years saw a great deal of fighting both in Uganda and on the line of the railway. There was constant trouble with Mwanga and he was eventually deposed by Colonel Ternan the British Acting-Commissioner. His one-year-old son Daudi Chwa was proclaimed Kabaka with his father's *Katikiro* Apollo Kagwa as Regent. Kagwa co-operated whole-heartedly with the British and soon established himself in a position of great power. His loyalty was absolute, he led the Baganda in several campaigns against their enemies and was instrumental in putting down a mutiny amongst the Sudanese troops. During the campaign against Bunyoro in 1893–94 Semei Kakungura, a Muganda, had distinguished himself and a great rivalry developed between himself and Apollo Kagwa. Kakungura realised it would be dangerous to stay in Kampala, so he retired to the Chiefdom of Bugerere which was part of his reward. From this base he struck northwards bringing the outer tribes under control; in this work he had the full backing of Colonel Ternan who made him chief of all the lands in the north. Kakungura built up a network of forts and strong points connected with good roads and appointed trusted Baganda to act as sub-chiefs of the conquered tribes. This policy of placing Baganda in authority over other tribes was one that was to be followed by the British and it led to the great power the Baganda eventually obtained in Uganda.

Until 1902 the Uganda Protectorate stretched eastwards to the Kedong River just under the Rift Valley escarpment near Nairobi, but then the whole of what had been the Eastern Province of Uganda was transferred to the East African Protectorate and the boundary between the two countries became as it is now. By this time the railway had been built from the Coast to Lake Victoria. Some of the difficulties and dangers of the work are described later but as a feat of engineering it was a wonderful achievement. After climbing to nearly 7,000 feet the line dropped into the Rift Valley by crawling down the side of the escarpment, it then crossed the valley floor, past volcanic cones, salt lakes and boiling mud, to climb up to the Mau Summit at 9,000 feet, the highest point on any colonial railway line, then down again to the shores of the lake. The whole operation had taken just over six years and in October 1903 the line was transferred from the Foreign Office to the East African Protectorate Administration.

Although the railway was originally planned as a link to Uganda, it soon became obvious that it would have to be paid for by the exploitation of the potential of land along its route.

22 A pony of the East African Mounted Rifles being camouflaged as a zebra during the campaign in the open veld around Kilimanjaro

Early travellers had remarked on the pleasantness of the country and its suitability for settlement. Lord Delamere, who first saw the country in 1897 on a safari from Ethiopia, was an ardent champion of settlement by Europeans and from 1903 he threw himself whole-heartedly into the development of the country. At first settlement was very slow, but in 1908 a flood of South Africans entered the country to take up wheat farming on the rolling plains above the Rift Escarpment, and in 1910 there was a similar influx of British colonists, most of whom had substantial capital backing unlike the Boers who came with animals and tools but little money. The necessity of alienating land quickly in order to satisfy the demands of the new settlers led to much immediate resentment and was, in the long run, the cause of deep disaffection. The effect of the Government's land policy on the Kikuyu and Masai is dealt with in the chapters devoted to these tribes, but their decision to reserve farmland solely for European occupation and to exclude Indians from settling as farmers was a source of just as great resentment.

By 1914 both Uganda and the East African Protectorate were economically fairly stable. Agriculture had increased to the point where it made a significant contribution to the revenue of the countries. Uganda was set on the path of development of African resources guided by a small band of European officials dedicated to the policies of indirect rule. Kenya (as the East African Protectorate was soon to be called) had become settler-dominated with a very powerful non-governmental lobby that commanded almost universal support amongst the Europeans. In German East Africa a strong government was developing the country as fast as possible, combining European plantation agriculture with African peasant cultivation of cash crops. Zanzibar, once at the centre of affairs and the focus of European attention, had slipped quietly into the status of Protectorate, her wealth firmly based on her clove and coconut plantations and her dhow trade with Arabia and India.

At the outbreak of war there were very few troops on either side in East Africa. Germany was in the more favourable position as she had nearly 3,000 officers and other ranks under the command of General Paul von Lettow-Vorbeck. He was an extremely able and experienced soldier, having fought in the Boxer Rebellion in China and then in South-West Africa and the Cameroons. Tropical warfare was no novelty to him. The British forces were already committed to actions against the Turkana, the Maretan, and to garrison duties

23   The *Königsberg* sunk in the Rufiji River

in the Northern Frontier District and Zanzibar. There were, in fact, only three and a half companies of the King's African Rifles uncommitted, and no headquarters staff at all. There was, however, an immediate response by the settler population, who formed a mounted regiment and one of infantry. The naval forces in East African waters were much stronger. The Germans had the modern light cruiser *Königsberg*, and the British the cruisers *Astrea*, *Hyacinth* and *Pegasus*. The *Königsberg* put to sea before the declaration of war and coaled in the Indian Ocean. She hunted for merchant ships in the western sector of the Ocean and coaled again at the end of August. After hiding for a few days in the mouth of the Rufiji River she raided Zanzibar and destroyed *Pegasus*. She was by now very short of fuel so headed back to the Rufiji to hide. Here she was discovered and blockaded, but due to her shallow draught she retreated farther up the river thwarting her pursuers who could not follow her. The blockade was maintained for nearly a year until two shallow-draught gunboats with high-trajectory guns able to lob shells over the intervening forest sailed out from England. The gunboats, the *Severn* and the *Mersey*, commenced the bombardment on 11 July 1915, and finally succeeded in sinking the *Königsberg*. Her crew had had time to dismount all her guns and ammunition and these made a very welcome addition to the fire-power of the land forces.

Von Lettow-Vorbeck knew that no action fought in East Africa could be decisive in the war as a whole, but if he could tie down as many troops as possible it would prevent these troops being used in the European theatre. With Britain, Portugal and Belgium as allies German East Africa was surrounded, but von Lettow-Vorbeck realised that the Uganda Railway was extremely vulnerable where it ran parallel to the frontier, from Mombasa to Machako's village. He therefore concentrated his forces around Kilimanjaro where there was ample food and from this base made raids across the border, cutting the railway many times and capturing the frontier town of Taveta.

The British countered the threat from Kilimanjaro by mounting an attack on Tanga to take von Lettow-Vorbeck in the rear. They launched the attack on 3 November 1914. The Germans resisted bravely and were reinforced next day by the troops from Kilimanjaro. Very heavy fighting took place all that day and on 5 November the British forces retreated, leaving very many casualties. The victory was completed by the rout of the right flank of the pincer movement (formed by a British column advancing round the flank of the Kilimanjaro positions) at Longido. Having failed to take Tanga from the sea the British advanced down the coast road from Mombasa and occupied Jassini. Von Lettow-Vorbeck counterattacked, hoping that more reinforcements would be sent to help the troops so that he could ambush them on the coast road, but after two days of heavy fighting the troops in Jassini surrendered. This second German victory was a severe blow to the morale of the British troops, but it had cost the Germans fairly heavy casualties and von Lettow-Vorbeck withdrew his forces to the pleasant climate of Kilimanjaro where they could recover and continue their guerrilla warfare along the Uganda railway line.

By 1916 the British had been reinforced by troops from India and South Africa and the command of them had been given to the famous Boer leader General Jan Christian Smuts. His plan was to deliver a two-pronged attack on the German forces, one column moving through Taveta to take the eastern side of the mountain, the other round Longido to take the Germans in the rear. In February the attacks were mounted and there was a period of heavy fighting. Smuts hoped that von Lettow-Vorbeck would stand and fight so that a decisive victory would finish the Germans as a force, but this was just what von Lettow-Vorbeck would not do. When the pressure became too much he withdrew first to Kahé, then across the Pangani River, fighting all the way. Here the rains gave him a breathing spell for the British drive had petered out and he could rest his weary troops.

At the same time as Smuts thrust from Taveta there were two other columns advancing into German territory. In the west the Belgians crossed the Congo frontier and occupied Ruanda; here they were joined by the British and the combined forces pushed on to capture the lake port of Mwanza, then turned southwards to Tabora and the Central Railway. In the south General Northey advanced from the Nyasaland-Rhodesia border, captured Tukuyu and pushed northwards towards Iringa.

Von Lettow-Vorbeck was not drawn into dispersing his forces to meet these various threats. He concentrated on the one area and continued to harass Smuts, refusing to be drawn into a set-piece battle but constantly worrying at the column by skirmishing and standing to fight whenever there was a favourable bit of ground. Having inflicted as many casualties as possible he disengaged his forces to repeat the whole manœuvre again. Slowly he fell back down the Tanga line, then turned south past the Uluguru mountains. Once again Smuts expected von Lettow-Vorbeck to stand and fight for the Central Railway line but he slipped south while Smuts had to halt the pursuit to rest his troops, many of whom were unable to move farther because of disease. When Nigerian and East African reinforcements arrived Smuts pushed on across the Rufiji River, but he was engaged in some very heavy fighting before he crossed the river. He then relinquished his command – saying the campaign in East Africa was finished and left for England! The next five months were periods of recuperation for both forces; the British were preparing to push inland from the ports of Kilwa and Lindi, the Germans were drawing together in a compact and highly mobile column. When the two-pronged assault from the west came, von Lettow-Vorbeck was ready and although he was facing overwhelming odds, including bombing aircraft, he inflicted heavy casualties on the attackers. As the sheer weight of numbers piled up he withdrew inland along the Ruvuma, and in November 1917 crossed into Portuguese East Africa. For the next year he led the forces against him a long and protracted chase, inflicting as heavy casualties as he could before disappearing into the bush. He drew the British after him to the south of Portuguese territory, at Quilimane, then outgeneralling them completely swung northwards so that he was between them and the Ruvuma. In September 1918 von Lettow-Vorbeck crossed back into German territory, but instead of carrying on northwards he swung round again, entered British territory in Northern Rhodesia and attacked the town of Fife.

On 13 November 1918 he was told of the Armistice. He was also told, quite untruthfully, that the terms of the Armistice included the unconditional surrender of his forces, and on 25 November he formally capitulated to General Edwards at Abercorn. His total force consisted of 155 Europeans and 4,227 Africans, of whom 819 were women. With this minute force, badly armed and chronically short of food and money, he had fulfilled his object, engaging forces often ten times as numerous as his own and keeping a large British effort pinned down in East Africa. His army had campaigned in the old style, living off the land, making their equipment from hides they shot and their medicines by boiling bark and herbs that they found. Describing the scene the *Bulawayo Chronicle* said:

'Von Lettow, whose striking presence is a good index of what must be a wonderful personality, came in at the head of his first detachment. . . . It was a most impressive spectacle. The long motley column, Europeans and Askaris, all veterans of a hundred fights, the latter clothed in every kind of headgear, women who had stuck to their husbands through all these years of hardship, carrying huge loads, some with children born during the campaign, carriers coming in singing in undisguised joy at the thought that their labours were ended at last.'

Von Lettow-Vorbeck surrendered but was given the full honours of war, he and his officers being allowed to keep their arms; it was the least acknowledgment that could have been made to this small, unconquered force. It is typical of von Lettow-Vorbeck that he immediately threw himself into the details of getting all his men repatriated and paid their arrears of pay.

There was a period of some uncertainty as to the future status of German East Africa but this was resolved when Britain accepted the mandate over the territory from the League of Nations. The old German provinces of Ruanda and Urundi were taken over by the Belgians and the boundary fixed as the line of the Kagera River. In order to prevent confusion between the two areas that it now governed, Britain named the old British portion of East Africa Kenya, the German portion Tanganyika.

Although the three countries had many problems in common and were all subject to the same economic ups and downs in the inter-war period, their political development varied tremendously. In Kenya the years after the war saw a great increase in the power of

24  Von Lettow-Vorbeck entertaining his staff. A photograph taken
in Dar-es-Salaam at the beginning of the war

the white settlers, ably and bigotedly led by Lord Delamere. The Convention of Associations, which was the central co-ordinating body of all the local colonists' associations, was known as the Settlers' Parliament and debated at great length measures proposed by the Government. For many years it called senior Government officials before it to explain their work and the Governor, in opening it, used the opportunity to announce major policy decisions. The settlers were dedicated to the achievement of full self-government as soon as possible; they were impatient of control from Whitehall and rejected utterly the notion that Africans or Indians should have any say in the government of the country. The Indian community was extremely dissatisfied with the representation allotted them on the Legislative Council and made many representations to London, while at the same time the settlers were pressing for the grant of self-government, using Southern Rhodesia as their example.

The matter was settled to no one's satisfaction by the White Paper issued in 1923 that stated categorically that responsible self-government was out of the question for the foreseeable future. The Indians were offered a chance to elect five members to the Council on a communal roll, but as the settlers were given eleven seats they remained dissatisfied. The troubled political waters were disturbed by the increasing activity of the Africans who were conscious of the injustices being done to them and needed an organisation comparable to the Convention of Associations to voice their grievances. The first of these was the Kikuyu Central Association, founded in 1920, but it was dominated by the chiefs who were paid Government servants, so did not inspire any confidence. In 1921 Harry Thuku founded the Young Kikuyu Association to fight the settlers' proposals for reducing the wages payable to Africans. The Association submitted a list of grievances to the British Government, by-passing the chiefs. Thuku worked tirelessly to extend the movement, talking to the tribes by the lake as well as the Kikuyu. He was arrested in 1922 and deported, but his work lived

41

on in the Young Kavirondo Association, whilst the Young Kikuyu Association reappeared as the Kikuyu Central Association. In 1930 the K.C.A. sent its secretary, Jomo Kenyatta, to England to present the African case. One of the results of this visit was the release of Thuku who was allowed to return from exile. He was elected President of the K.C.A. in 1932. There was increasing political activity for the rest of the decade with many African parties being formed and grievances being aired more and more openly.

In Tanganyika the Legislative Council was created with very little fuss and there was steady progress, unmarred by the bitternesses of Kenya. It was in the field of administration that Tanganyika broke new ground. Sir Donald Cameron was appointed Governor in 1924, having previously been Chief Secretary in Northern Nigeria. Here he had become well grounded in the Lugard philosophy of 'indirect rule' and it was his intention to introduce it to Tanganyika. The mandate from the League of Nations was looked on as 'a sacred trust' and in his *Dual Mandate in British Tropical Africa* Lord Lugard had crystallised the ideas that were then current, to lead the country forward both economically and politically until it could stand on its own.

Cameron was a remarkable man; having started life as a post office sorter in British Honduras he had come to the top in the Colonial Service. In his work he was ably assisted by Philip Mitchell (later knighted and appointed Governor of Uganda and then Governor of Kenya) who admits that the devotees of the theory of Indirect Rule 'were in some danger of becoming a sort of orgiastic order of monks'. The theory was basically quite simple – to administer the people through their own traditional tribal hierarchies, taking cognisance of native law and custom and building up at this level a knowledge of, and ability in, local government and finance that could be developed into an ability to administer the whole country. Patiently and slowly the local administration was set up, against apathy, against some peculation, against some knavery. As a system it worked well. It gave the people their own Treasuries, their own Native Courts and the ability to make their own bye-laws. Perhaps the greatest tribute to the system is the fact that when the time came for the transition from Colonial rule it ensured a peaceful change over because all the people already felt fully represented politically. It was in Kenya with its system of administration divorced from the bulk of the people, with chiefs paid as Government servants and so distrusted, that the breakdown of law and order came.

The administrative position in Uganda was complicated by the fact that Buganda and the other 'treaty' kingdoms enjoyed a special relationship with Britain. The Baganda did not consider their *Lukiko* (Parliament) a local government, to them it was a central government. There was not so definite a feeling in the other kingdoms but it was none the less there. When the Baganda who had been acting as local headmen in the non-Baganda areas were replaced by local men this was taken as a great step forward in 'indirect rule' but in reality it was no such thing for the new men were still government appointees.

The steady, if diverse, progress administratively was not matched economically in the inter-war years, boom and slump followed each other with sickening regularity. To the world depressions of 1921–2 and 1930–2 were added the local problems of severe drought and invasions of locusts. Economies that were at best precariously balanced found these repeated blows difficult to weather; the effects were severe retrenchments in the development

25 The end of the Italian Empire. The remnants of the Duke of Aosta's forces being accorded the honours of war as they surrender at Amba Alagi. The countryside is typical of the terrain over which this campaign was fought

programmes and the heartbreaking task of seeing cherished projects halted, perhaps abandoned for ever. Then just as all the territories were entering a period of economic prosperity came the Second World War.

The war had been long expected and caused little immediate disruption; except to the 3,200 German nationals in Tanganyika who were quickly interned, some for the second time.

Kenya had a frontier with Italy and as soon as war was declared between the countries British patrols started to raid over the Abyssinian border; they were soon pushed back and Moyale was occupied by the Italians. In January 1941 Wavell mounted the counter-attack that he hoped would finish the East African front once and for all. At the time the campaign was overshadowed by the news from the Western Desert, but now it is possible to see this as one of Wavell's best campaigns. He was brilliantly served by his two subordinate commanders, Cunningham and Platt, and despite a constant barrage of criticism, bad advice and ill-considered rebuke from Churchill, he persevered in his plans until his numerically small army destroyed the Italian Empire completely. In essence the campaign was a pincer movement. A great outflanking move on the right through Eritrea capturing the ports of Kismayu and Mogadishu was balanced by a thrust eastward from the Sudan aimed at the Red Sea. The pincer was supported by a drive through the centre of Ethiopia by partisan forces and a small contingent of British troops. The climax to the campaign was the battle for Keren, a town standing on a plateau, approached by a road in a deep gorge, commanded by heights on either side. It was considered an impregnable position and General Frusci, the Italian Commander, concentrated all his forces there. The fight has been called 'as hard a soldiers' battle as ever was fought'. The 4th Indian Division stormed the heights to clear the road and for five days the battle raged with no let-up, the heights being taken and lost twice by each side. Then a pause while the 5th Indian Division was brought up and another assault that captured the heights of Dologorudoc to the right of the road, finally the bloody push up the road itself with the defeat of the Italian garrison. With the fall of Keren there could be little doubt as to the end of the campaign; Cunningham pushed inland taking Harar and entering Addis Ababa on 6 April. The finale of the campaign occurred at Amba Alagi, a very strong defensive position which the 5th Indian Division attacked in May. After two days the Duke of Aosta surrendered and the campaign was over.

The campaign has been called 'a feat of spontaneous exploitation unsurpassed in war'. With exterior lines of communication stretching most of the time over a thousand miles of trackless desert and scrub, a small force had defeated and captured over 250,000 well trained and well equipped opponents and occupied over a million square miles of enemy territory. John Connell, Wavell's biographer, has written: 'In its strategic completeness the victory was Wavell's. His was the vision that created it, by careful planning, in the face of all the barrage of long-range adjuration; and his was the hand that steadied and guided this astonishing campaign, through every vicissitude, to that final ceremony at Amba Alagi.'

The Japanese entry into the war and their spectacular successes in the Pacific and south-east Asia posed a new threat to East Africa. It was possible that they might strike across the Indian Ocean, or perhaps enter Madagascar which was controlled by the Vichy French and who would not deny control of this vital island to Japan. Madagascar was therefore invaded in late 1942 by East African forces and quickly occupied.

After the war the years of plenty continued. Sisal, coffee and cotton were all booming, and development funds were made available for many essential projects. Some of the

26   Julius Nyerere, President of Tanzania

schemes were ill founded like the 'Groundnut scheme', a grandiose pipe-dream to grow these oil-bearing nuts by mechanised means that failed because no local pilot schemes were undertaken nor was local opinion consulted. In its later stages of wasteful extravagance the scheme had all the trappings of delusive fantasy as ex-army men and vehicles tried to farm with nothing but battle experience behind them. Other projects were far-seeing, such as the damming of the Nile at Owen Falls and the concentration on road and railway building in the three territories.

The stable economy was not matched by stable politics, except perhaps in Tanganyika, which had been placed by Ernest Bevin under the Trusteeship of the United Nations as soon as the Trusteeship Council had been formed. The triennial visits of the Council Members gave to Tanganyika a feeling of being specially cared for, acting as an assurance to the Africans that they were not forgotten in Africa but were in fact the centre of attention. Throughout the fifties the Tanganyika African National Union had been working to prepare the people for independence, led by Julius Nyerere. He was the son of a chief of the Zanaki tribe, educated at the Tabora Government School and Makerere College in Uganda. He taught for some time at Tabora and then in 1949 became the first Tanganyikan student to go to a British University. He graduated from Edinburgh University and returned to Tanganyika to enter politics. He took the old Tanganyika African Association and turned it into T.A.N.U., a party openly committed to the cause of Independence. Unlike the other countries of East Africa, Tanganyika prospered with one party (a European party dedicated to multi-racialism, the United Tanganyika Party, collapsed with the success of T.A.N.U.). In the 1960 elections to the Legislative Council all seats (including ten European and eleven Asian) were taken by T.A.N.U. candidates, and Julius Nyerere became Prime Minister; self-government was granted in May 1961 and Independence on 9 December of that year. The peaceful transition was a triumph for the personality of Nyerere and the strength of T.A.N.U. which had welded African, Indian and European into one party working for one goal. The resignation of Nyerere as Prime Minister on 22 January 1962 was therefore a complete shock to the outside world but, as always, Nyerere was acting in the best interests of his country – his explanation is given in his own words:

'This is the best way of achieving our new objective – the creation of a country in which the people take full and active part in the fight against poverty, ignorance and disease. To achieve this it is necessary to have an able elected government which has the full support and co-operation of the people. This we have had and will have. It is also necessary to have a strong political organisation, active in every village, which acts like a two-way all-weather road along which the purposes, plans, and problems of the Government can travel to the people at the same time the ideas, desires and misunderstandings of the people can travel direct to the Government. This is the job of the new T.A.N.U.'

It was Nyerere who had coined the phrase *Uhuru na Kazi* (Freedom and Work) before the elections and having achieved *Uhuru* he went back to the work he considered most important, the creation of a strong political machine reaching down to village level to back the Government in all it did. The wisdom of this decision was shown after the declaration

27  Modern boat-building techniques provide craft for the fishing
industry on Lake Victoria

of the Republic on 9 December 1962, when Nyerere assumed the office of President and
guided the new nation through the upheavals of the K.A.R. mutiny and the Zanzibar
Rebellion to eventual union with Zanzibar and the creation of the new state of Tanzania.

In Uganda the first of the major post-war troubles was the banishment of the Kabaka
Frederick Mutesa II in 1953. This event was the outcome of a long struggle in Uganda between the Baganda Parliament (the *Lukiko*) and the Legislative Council. Increases in the
African representation on the Council meant a serious weakening of Buganda's position in
Uganda and this resulted in a refusal by the *Lukiko* to co-operate with the Government. An
unwise remark by the Colonial Secretary, Oliver Lyttelton, was seized on by the Baganda,
who said it showed the Government's desire to federate East Africa against the wishes of
the Baganda and they demanded the placing of Buganda under Foreign Office control, pre-
paratory to granting independence. This claim the Kabaka supported and when he refused
to agree to the Government's proposals for a united Uganda he was deposed and deported
to Britain. In 1954 Sir Keith Hancock drafted a new constitution that increased African
representation in the Legislative Council to half the members and guaranteed that no
federation would be imposed without the full consent of all the people of Uganda. On these
terms the *Lukiko* agreed to co-operate and Mutesa returned to Kampala in triumph in
October 1955, having signed the new agreement. Unfortunately this was not the end of
constitutional problems, for the desire for a united Uganda was strongly opposed by many
Baganda who wished only for Buganda to become a federal state of Uganda. In the elections
of March 1961 the Democratic Party, led by Benedicto Kiwanuka, swept to power (due to

46

the boycott of the elections by the Baganda) and he became Prime Minister. With the announcement of further elections in 1962 to choose the representatives who would take over full self-government in that year, Kiwanuka found himself opposed by a coalition of two very strong parties, the *Kabaka Yeka* (Kabaka only) in Buganda and the Uganda Peoples Congress led by Milton Obote, a Lango from the north of Uganda. This coalition swept the board at the elections, the *Kabaka Yeka* taking every Baganda seat from the Democratic Party, and it was Milton Obote who led the country to Independence on 9 October 1962. The alliance between the two parties was always an uneasy one, founded not on a community of interests but a rigid policy of not opposing each other when there were clashes of principle. The inevitable end came in 1966 when the Kabaka's palace was attacked by troops under the order of Obote. The Kabaka managed to escape the holocaust and fled first to Ruanda and thence to Britain, while Obote consolidated his position in Uganda.

Kenya had been in the forefront of constitutional change, for in 1944 it had introduced the first African to sit in any East African Legislative Council. In 1945 the main departments of Government were placed in the care of Members of the Executive Council and in 1948 a Speaker presided over the Council in place of the Governor; in the same year there was a majority of unofficial members. Despite this the African representation was very low and there was great agitation amongst the Africans for further political advance. In 1946 Jomo Kenyatta returned to Kenya, having spent the war in Britain, working on the land and lecturing for the Workers Educational Association. Before the war he had studied in London and Birmingham, also for a time at Moscow University, working tirelessly for the cause of African rights. Soon after his return to Kenya he became President of the Kenya African Union, a mainly Kikuyu organisation. He quickly dominated the political scene. A superb orator, with a deep understanding of the tribes and their aspirations, he united the Africans in solid protest against European domination. His meetings were attended by thousands and by the early fifties he had such a hold on the people that the settlers were agitating for his deportation.

28  Jomo Kenyatta, President of Kenya

47

As passions grew and the highly literate and sophisticated Kikuyu found more and more frustrations in the way of achieving some form of political representation the acts of subversion and violence also grew. Arson and robbery became common in the Reserves. The numbers of terrorists grew, and gradually tales of solemn oath taking and the formation of bands pledged to fight to the death for the freedom of Kenya began to be current. In October 1952 a state of emergency was proclaimed and Kenyatta and five other K.A.U. leaders were arrested and charged with managing Mau Mau. In April 1953 he was sentenced to seven years imprisonment on this charge. Meanwhile the country had degenerated into civil war with Kikuyu fighting Kikuyu and British forces combing the forests of the Aberdares for the terrorist gangs who raided the villages and outlying European farms, butchering the occupants.

The true causes of Mau Mau may never be known; the line between the freedom fighter and the tribal savage is almost impossible to draw. The early years of the emergency were bestial and much was done by both sides that is best forgotten but perhaps, in the long run,

29  The National Assembly in session

the greatest damage done by Mau Mau was to the shape of African politics. Mau Mau was almost solely a Kikuyu movement so that when _Uhuru_ was achieved there was a tendency for the Kikuyu to take all the credit for it, to look on other tribes as ex-collaborators and almost 'second class citizens'. It is certain that the mainly tribal divisions in Kenya politics today are due to the tribal emphasis laid by the Mau Mau.

In 1960 the emergency was ended and a constitutional conference held in London to discuss the form of the new Legislative Council. At this time there emerged the two great African political parties that were to fight the forthcoming elections. The Kenya African National Union was composed of the Kikuyu, Kamba and Luo tribes and campaigned for independence and one state; the Kenya African Democratic Union composed of the smaller tribes also wanted independence but fearing domination by the Kikuyu they also wanted a federation of equal tribal states. Although in prison, Jomo Kenyatta continued to dominate the political scene. The kind of reverence in which he was held is well shown in the following extract from Josiah Kariuki's account of his visit to the detained Kenyatta given in his book _Mau Mau Detainee_:

'There, framed in the doorway, waiting for us, was _Mzee_. He greeted us in a wonderful manner and as he embraced me to him I felt like a tiny chicken being folded under its mother's wings; all my worries and troubles now belonged to him. This would be a small burden indeed for a man who had already taken the suffering of all our people on himself. . . . The living, throbbing, hustling, laughing, crying, bursting mass of our people love him more than anything [_sic_] else they know. He is our chosen leader and he alone will lead us out of the past, out of the deep pits of dark memories to the bright future of our country. . . . He is human and yet wiser than any other human being I have ever known. They are all his people, his responsibility, and his children; all fellow human beings to love and to cherish, to correct if they do wrong, to praise if they do right.'

In 1960 he was elected (while still detained) President of K.A.N.U. and when the Governor refused to register it as a legal organisation James Gickeru took the Presidency declaring he would vacate it as soon as Kenyatta was released. In August he was released but barred from entering Legislative Council as he had served more than two years in prison. This bar was raised in November 1961 when the constitution of Kenya was amended and on 13 January 1962, having been returned unopposed for the Fort Hall constituency the day before, Jomo Kenyatta took his seat in the Council as Leader of the Opposition. In 1963 K.A.N.U. triumphed at the polls and Kenyatta became the first Prime Minister of Kenya, becoming President when full independence was granted to the country. Since that time he has transformed Kenya. A man of outstanding presence he gained first the respect and later the trust of the Europeans. He guided the country through the first years of independence, never allowing nationalism to get out of hand, always steering the country towards unity. A cross between patriarch and elder statesman he is called _Mzee_ by everyone – a Swahili honorific bestowed as a mark of respect on elders – slowly but surely he has taken thirty-two tribes and three races and welded them by his vision and his strength into one people, one nation; standing like a rock in the troubled sea of African affairs.

# 4 Coastal and Upland peoples of Kenya

CENTURIES OF RULE BY THE ARABS have left their mark on the coastal peoples of East Africa, making them more cosmopolitan than the inland African. They have imposed a standard of culture along the whole of the Coast that allows a person from Lamu in the north to feel at home and able to converse in the same language with a dweller in the far south. Inland, a journey of this length would cross many tribal and ethnic frontiers and there would be no similarities between the start and end of the journey.

Within this general similarity of background lie bewildering strata of castes. At the top there is the Arab trader, owner of the local store and coconut plantations, the local transport contractor, running lorries and a bus to the nearest district centre. Next is the 'Swahili', a Muslim, wearing a long white robe and embroidered cap, often with a decorated waist-coat. He speaks the pure language of the Coast, often using Arabic phrases and intonations. Then there is the local fisherman, usually of Bantu origin, but often with Arab blood, forming a quite separate group from the Africans who also live in the coastal strip but who farm the land. Many of these farmers have emigrated from their tribal areas and settled in the fertile plain, while some are the descendants of slaves brought down to the Coast.

The sea, of course, dominates the lives of the coastal dwellers, for not only does it provide fish for food, but the land also depends on the monsoon winds to bring the rains that make crop cultivation possible. It is when the monsoons change from south-east to north-east in November and December, and back again in April, that the main rains occur, but there are no months completely without rain. The whole of the Coast, with the exception of the very northern portion above Lamu, receives over forty inches of rain per year and this rises to sixty inches in parts of the off-shore islands.

The fisherman has a hard, long day with very little return for his labour. Although the sea is swarming with fish, the physical conditions are such that large hauls are not possible without expensive equipment. The whole of the Coast is composed of coral, a rock created by myriads of small sea creatures. The coral grows upward to the limit of the tide and then dies and solidifies while new coral grows on the seaward side – the land is thus pushing constantly out to sea and from the shore there is often a walk of half a mile to the water's edge at low tide. Beyond the edge of the reef there are large detached corals growing from the sandy bottom and it is these, with their razor-sharp edges, that make any form of trawling impossible in these waters, for they quickly tear any net to shreds. The fisherman, therefore, has to use either hand lines or basket traps in the coral to catch his fish.

At low tide the fisherman sets out in his *ungalaua*, the outrigger canoe that is standard throughout the area. The hull is made from a log (mango wood being the favourite as it is extremely tough and does not rot in the sea) hollowed out and shaped so that it is just wide enough for one person. Two poles are then fixed across the boat projecting several feet on

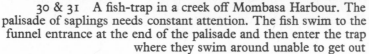

30 & 31    A fish-trap in a creek off Mombasa Harbour. The
palisade of saplings needs constant attention. The fish swim to the
funnel entrance at the end of the palisade and then enter the trap
where they swim around unable to get out

either side and to these cross bars flat outrigger blades are attached to stabilise the boat
laterally. A mast made from a mangrove pole is stepped in the fore part of the central hull
and on this a lateen sail is set carried on a bamboo yard. The *ungalaua* is ideally suited to its
work, drawing only a few inches; it is light enough to paddle easily, sails very fast on or off
the wind and has a large capacity for nets, lines, traps and fish.

There are three ways of catching fish off the reef and many of the fishermen will try all
of them in a day. For the large rock-cod and other bottom-feeding fish the boat is allowed
to drift gently with the incoming tide, while the fishermen use a baited hand line to hook
the fish. The reef fish can also be caught in basket traps baited with small pieces of fish and
crushed crabs and sea urchins. The traps have a funnel entrance and once the fish enters it
cannot find the way out. Any crabs or small fish found in the baskets when they are hauled
up are used as bait for the next set. In addition to the bottom feeders, there are the pelagic
or surface-feeding fish, including such game fish as the marlin, sailfish, barracuda, tunny
and horse mackerel. They are caught by trolling a silver spoon or a live bait behind a swiftly
moving boat. At certain seasons, when the small sardines are running, heavy catches are
possible as the tunny come after them. At such times the fish seem to go mad and they can
be caught on a hook baited with a small piece of red rag.

51

32 Fishing boats drawn up on the beach after the day's work. The sails are left up to dry as the catch is unloaded

Four or five hours of hard work will usually yield the fisherman twenty or thirty pounds of fish; then with the turn of the tide he makes for land, where he either sells his fish to the village trader, or sets off inland himself with the fish in a basket on his bicycle to sell the catch to the farmers.

In addition to these general ways of fishing there are three specialised methods. The principle of the basket is extended to the construction of large fish traps that jut out a hundred yards from the shore. The traps are constructed in creeks or inlets where the ground is sandy and will take easily the saplings and withies used in making the traps. With the rise and fall of the tide, fish swimming parallel to the shore are deflected by the arm of the trap and swim along it until they enter the compartment at the end through a narrow funnel. There they are trapped and can be taken out by hand at low tide.

Shark is a great delicacy all over East Africa, prized for its acrid flavour and the fact that a very small portion of dried shark will flavour a whole bowl of maize meal. Small sharks are often caught when bottom fishing for reef fish, but for the larger ones (weighing anything up to 400 pounds) a special shark line is set. A heavy hook attached to a strong chain is baited with a goat's bowels or head, or the head of a large fish. The chain is hung from a buoy made from a petrol drum, which is in turn anchored with a strong rope. The bait is left in a channel where shark are known to swim. When the shark is hooked he tires himself out fighting against the buoyancy of the drum, and the fisherman can go out in the morning

52

and easily bring him in. The same principle of letting the shark tire itself by fighting is achieved by leading the line ashore and making it fast to the top of a palm tree; the spring in the trunk absorbs all the fight of the shark.

Another great delicacy is *dagaa*, small dried fish the size of sardines. These are caught by net, either by casting a circular net over a shoal from a boat or by rowing a net out from shore, circling a shoal and hauling both ends of the net to the shore, with the catch securely bagged.

On land, the main produce of the coastal strip is copra. This is the dried inside of the coconut, from which is pressed coconut oil. The nuts grow from the crown of leaves at the top of the trunk and are harvested by men who climb the trunk and cut the nuts down. The act of climbing to this height up a thin swaying trunk seems to exhilarate the harvesters for they shout and sing at their work, laughing and racing each other up and down trees, so that when a plantation is being harvested it sounds as though the trees are full of a flock of very large birds, chattering, screaming and singing amongst the dark fronds.

Copra is not the only product of the coconut palm. The leaves are woven into a form of thatch called *makuti* which is still the main roofing material in the villages. Individual leaves of the palm are used to weave mats, bags and baskets, and the milk of a green coconut, drunk fresh from the tree on a hot, humid, sweltering day, is a drink for the Gods.

From the dank areas of mangrove swamp along the Coast comes a harvest of poles. They are particularly prized in Arabia which has no usable timber of its own and form one of the main cargoes carried by the sea-going dhows on their journey back to Muscat. The poles are also used extensively for scaffolding and in the building of the traditional mud and wattle huts of the Coast.

Because of the rainfall and the general fertility of the soil, the coastal strip is one of the most densely populated parts of East Africa, particularly the section from Mombasa south

33 Pillar tombs and a ruined mosque at Malindi. In the background can be seen the sweep of the bay

to Dar-es-Salaam, with the heaviest concentration occurring round Tanga. A wide range of food is grown, the staple crops being maize and cassava, a tuberous root crop from which a flour is made rather like arrowroot. In addition to these staples, peas, rice, bananas, cashew nuts and citrus fruits also grow easily. Muheza, inland from Tanga, is famous for its oranges, the original trees being brought from China by the Arab traders. When the *San Raphael* was wrecked on the reef south of Tanga on Vasco da Gama's return voyage from India he noted the fine quality and juicy sweetness of the oranges that were brought out to him from the shore. There is a lush greenness and prosperity about the Coast, with goats and chickens scattering about the huts, ample food growing in the gardens and small-holdings, and spare cash coming into every family from the sale of coconuts, cashew nuts and citrus.

Along the Coast are towns that contain some of the greatest contrasts in East Africa, where modern concrete rubs shoulders with ancient coral and lime. Malindi is perhaps the best example. Visited by the Chinese in the early fifteenth century when it was known as Ma-lin, colonised by the Portuguese, mentioned by Milton, it has a cross erected by Vasco da Gama on his first visit and old pillar tombs that were nearly a hundred years old when da Gama landed. But Malindi is also the holiday resort for Kenya, with large modern luxury hotels jostling the old Arab town. The popularity of Malindi stems from the fact that the bay is a long curve of bare sand, without the usual coral reef. This means that the swimming is safe and pleasant, it also means that the large Indian Ocean swell can roll right inshore, giving fine surfing. Across the bay are lagoons and coral inlets teeming with brightly coloured fish and sea plants that give some of the finest underwater goggling in the world.

34   The waterfront at Lamu

North of Malindi, just below the border with Somaliland, is the Lamu Archipelago, a cluster of islands that stretch along the Coast. The largest of the islands is Paté, once a thriving port and the seat of an independent sultanate, now a neglected cluster of small huts with the ruins of the old palace and gateway standing forlorn and overgrown. Lamu, built on the next island, is the only surviving completely Arabic town on the Coast. A huge lethargy envelops it; the only movement is the dancing flicker of sunlight reflected from the sea and the ceaseless rocking of the boats tied up in front of the wharf. The town sleeps in the heat behind heavily carved doors, merchants doze in the backs of dim shops; nothing of the present obtrudes into what appears to be a film set for the production of a story from the *Arabian Nights*. At the peak of its power Lamu rivalled Mombasa, having a fine natural harbour and a plentiful supply of sweet water. It was famous for the building of fine ships, and there is still some ship-building carried on in the Archipelago. Apart from this the town lives on the export of mangrove poles, copra, coir and dried fish. Lamu exists in a timeless world, neither wanting progress nor seeking change. James Kirkman, the archaeologist who has uncovered so much of East Africa's Arabic past, says of Lamu, 'Unregenerate, grasping, perverted, polite and profoundly suspicious – it is refreshing to find one place in the world that does not pretend to believe in progress or indeed in motion at all.'

South of Malindi lie the ruins of Gedi. There is some mystery as to why Gedi was built where it was, for it is four miles from the sea and two miles from a navigable creek with an extremely tricky entrance. There is also no apparent reason for the abandonment of such a large and prosperous town, though Kirkman has suggested it might be due to the drying-up of the wells in the sixteenth century. For centuries the ruins lay crumbling in the forest, visited by no one as the place had a reputation for ghosts and apparitions. In the last fifteen years the site has been cleared, the walls made safe, so that visitors may wander the streets of this old town and peer into deserted courtyards and palaces that were once filled with bustling life. Gedi is a strange and powerful place, everyone who visits it talks of the aura and the feeling of being an intruder.

At Kilwa there is a feeling of a leisured and patrician civilisation. All that is now left of the oldest and most highly cultured of the Arab city states is a ruined group of castles, mosques and a palace; but amongst these ruins are some of the finest examples of medieval building in East Africa. The Great Mosque has eighteen domes supported on octagonal pillars with high barrel-vaults between. Many of the other domes are decorated with bowls of white porcelain set into the plaster and even at this remove of time it is apparent that the standard of decoration was of a richness that was unmatched elsewhere on the Coast. A recent excavation of one of the castles has shown it to have been more luxurious than anything else so far excavated. It has a series of open courts leading to an octagonal pool with living rooms opening from the enclosures. In the ruins of Kilwa one can feel reflected the culture and leisure of the Persian city of Shiraz, which was its parent and which so obviously moulded its life; just as the courtyards, shops and functional mosques of Gedi reflect the economic pragmatism of the Muscat traders who built it.

The coastal strip, besides supporting a thriving population and containing a wealth of archaeological sites, also has some of the finest natural harbours in the world, some as yet not used at all. Mombasa and Dar-es-Salaam will be examined in detail later. Tanga, which

55

35  A fisherman with two of the
brightly coloured fish that live in
the coral reefs

36  An Arab hunter settled near
Kilosa. The charm on the chain is
made from the claw of a lion

is the entrepôt for the rich hinterland of plantations and farms that reaches inland to Kilimanjaro, is a perfect circle, entered through a narrow channel and completely protected by
land on all sides.

Pangani – the *Rhapta* of Ptolemy – lies on the north bank of its eponymous river. A
place of some importance in the past, it was ceded to Germany by Seyyid Bargash in 1886.
A large custom-house and fort were built to dominate the town and plantations were started
in the surrounding country. Between Pangani and Dar-es-Salaam is Bagamoyo – a town
that still seems oppressed by the load of sorrow it has engendered. It has an excellent dhow
harbour, a gentle sandy bay where the large ocean-going dhows can be beached in perfect
safety, a great number of fine Arab doorways and solid old buildings of the original German
Government which used Bagamoyo as the capital of their East African Protectorate.

South of Dar-es-Salaam are the three Kilwas: Kilwa Kisiwani ('Kilwa on the island'),
Kilwa Kivinje ('Kilwa of the casuarina trees'), and Kilwa Masoko ('Kilwa where shellfish
are dug'). The name Kilwa derives from the Swahili word *Kelele* – a noise, and legend has
it that when Arabs attacked the island in the eleventh century the inhabitants hid along the
Coast and on the approach of the Arabs sang and intoned prayers so loudly that the Arabs
were deceived as to their numbers, and abandoned the attack. Kilwa Kisiwani – the 'Quiloa'
of Milton – was a town rich and prosperous before the Portuguese came to the Coast;
Kilwa Kivinje was the old headquarters for the district, while Kilwa Masoko, the new headquarters, is built on the tip of a peninsula that looks over one of the finest harbours on the
Coast.

In the far south are the ports of Lindi and Mtwara. Lindi – which means 'deep water'
in Swahili – is an important port, handling an export trade of timber and local produce from
the interior, while Mtwara (meaning 'a carrier off of another man's wife', a reference to a
legendary escapade of a local chief) is a new port that was built to serve the farming area of

56

Nachingwea, to which it is united by railway. It has a future importance as the alternative port for the shipment of Zambian copper if the Rhodesian railway remains closed.

The Africans who live in the upland areas of Kenya are the descendants of the Bantu who pushed westward from the Congo forests about two thousand years ago. They did not at once occupy the land on which they are now living, for they have tribal legends that place their origins to the east of their present areas. There must have been a period of wandering and fighting between the Bantu and the primitive Bushmen before the groups settled down. From this original stock have sprung four main groups, the Kikuyu, Embu and Meru, who are inter-related and have a common language, and the Wakamba, who for many years were their enemies.

When these tribes first settled in Kenya the whole of the upland area from Mount Kenya to the edge of the Rift Valley was covered in dense forest. It was country quite like that of the Congo from whence they came, where they could practise the shifting cultivation to which they were accustomed. In this system, common to the whole of Africa south of the Sahara, a family occupies a portion of virgin forest, cutting down the undergrowth and burning the trees to clear a patch of land. The clearing is then cultivated until its goodness is exhausted, when the family moves on to another patch and starts the process all over again. In spite of the dense cover and luxuriant growth, soil depth over most of the forest areas of Africa is thin and very soon exhausted. The reason for this is that the vegetation is in a state of balance with the soil. The trees and bushes drop their leaves, which rot into a humus, which in turn feeds the trees. In the Congo forests it has been calculated that nearly twenty-five tons of leaves and small branches fall on each acre per year. The balance is so fine, however, that the whole of the humus is consumed by the tree and hardly any soil is formed. Once the forest cover is burnt off there remains a shallow layer of soil which is quickly impoverished and becomes almost sterile. The exhaustion is hastened by the heavy rainfall in the highlands which washes away the lime and nutrient salts, leaving the soil acid and useless. When the clan moves on to cultivate another patch the area they have cleared takes a very long time to regenerate – if indeed it ever does so.

In primitive societies there seem to have been forces that held the numbers of the population in an equilibrium with the capacity of the environment in which they lived. These forces did not operate with the Kikuyu whose numbers steadily increased throughout the centuries. From the slopes of Mount Kenya, which they revered as the home of their God *Ngai*, they spread northwards past Nyeri until they were halted by the Masai; then they spread westwards to the edge of the Rift escarpment where again they were stopped by the Masai; they spread up the slopes of the Aberdares until they were stopped by the cold and the altitude; finally they crossed the Chania River and spread south leaving a fringe of forest as a buffer between themselves and the open plains where the Masai roamed. This was the limit of their territory, for to the east were the Wakamba, with a no-man's-land and battleground between them running south from what is now Fort Hall. The Kikuyu had reached these limits by the end of the nineteenth century and they were beginning to feel the real pressure of an exploding population when a calamitous outbreak of smallpox in 1890 relieved, for a time, the pressure.

The tribal structure of the Kikuyu developed as they spread over the highlands. They

57

had no 'King' or single Paramount Chief. They organised themselves as family units that developed into a loose clan system. It was the family that cleared new ground and who considered themselves the 'owner' of this ground, but they were willing to let off portions of their holding to outsiders who needed land; yet this leased land was always retained in the overall ownership of the family. As numbers increased parts of the family would move to new areas, founding a sub-clan which still felt bound by the strongest ties to its parents. The cross-bonds so forged were strengthened by the age-set system, which bound together all the children of a certain age in a special relationship as comprehensive as a blood-tie.

On the clan system was superimposed a system of local confederation to deal with the communal affairs of the district. As the Kikuyu lived in the highlands, their districts were demarcated by the river valleys that cut the land into long ridges. It was these ridges, running at right angles to the axis of the Aberdares, that became the basic units of government. On each ridge there grew up a council of men elected from the families that lived along the ridge. The councils had overall authority in their district, but there was no one person in single authority. Decisions were arrived at after full debate; they might be implemented by one councillor; but no person on the council was pre-eminent. One of the gravest mistakes of the British was to try to impose upon this pattern of democratic government a system of chiefs totally foreign to the basic ethos of the Kikuyu.

By the time that the Kikuyu had recovered from the epidemic of smallpox a limit had been set to any further southward expansion. The British Government had drawn a line along the edge of the land at that time occupied by the Kikuyu and had declared all the land outside that boundary 'Crown Land'. This was land vested in the Government and available for settlement by Europeans. The actual land taken from the Kikuyu was not great, as in fact it was not occupied. What caused dissension then and proved to be a continuing source of grievance was the limitation of the Kikuyu's right to use as much land as he needed to provide for himself and his family. The creation of 'Native Reserves' and 'Crown Lands' was a violation of a basic concept of African thought which did not recognise the ownership of unoccupied land. Land was there to be used, like water or air, and should be as freely available. It was not land that was stolen, it was the tribes' futurity.

The population pressure that built up within the Reserves had two outlets – emigration to work in the growing township of Nairobi, or to the new farms. On the farms there grew up a system of tenure that came to be known as the 'squatter system'. The African was allowed to build his hut on the farm and bring his family to live with him, he was allotted a piece of land to cultivate for his own needs and allowed to pasture a stated number of sheep or goats on the farm. In return he was employed on a casual basis for the farmwork, being paid a low wage in return for the right of 'squatting' on the farm. It was a feudal system and had the advantages and disadvantages inherent in such a relationship. The farmer often provided medical care of a rudimentary kind for all the squatters, a school for their children and light work for the women. On the debit side was the overcrowding in the huts, which were limited in number, so that natural increases in the family had to be accommodated in the existing huts; but perhaps the worst feature was the feeling engendered in the squatters of living on sufferance on land that should in their view have been used by their tribe. To add to this sense of grievance there was the fact that many of the farms were extremely badly

37  A typical erosion gully in Ukamba

run – either through ignorance or through poverty. Many of the settlers had sunk every penny they possessed into buying their farms. Between the wars, as crops failed and the world economic situation deteriorated, the farmers got deeper and deeper into debt. Many were crippled by mortgages and overdrafts; they were reduced to bare subsistence farming to feed themselves and their families. Farms that would have carried three or four thousand Africans were, in Kikuyu eyes, wasted on a few privileged Europeans growing crops that the African was prohibited from planting for himself.

In the Reserves the numbers continued to grow. As the land was subjected to greater pressures, it began to deteriorate. Indiscriminate planting on the steep hillsides resulted in two forms of erosion: 'sheet erosion' where the whole topsoil is washed away by a heavy fall of rain, and 'gully erosion' where the water cuts deeper and deeper into the earth as it runs off the bare hillsides. Not only was the land having to feed more and more people, it was also losing its fertility. It was, paradoxically, the Mau Mau emergency that led to the changing of the squatter system and the improvement of the Kikuyu lands. Prior to the emergency very little notice was taken by the Kikuyu of agricultural advice given to them by the officers of the Government. Under the emergency powers, chiefs obtained much greater control over the population, and soil conservation works such as terracing and the filling in of erosion gullies were carried out under the orders of the Government as works urgently necessary to increase the food production of the Reserves to cope with the thousands of squatters who were returned from the European farms. The ending of Kikuyu squatting was nearly always a voluntary act on the part of the squatters. In an attempt to control the movement of the Kikuyu and to prevent their aiding the hard-core fighters in the forests, the Government made remaining a farm squatter conditional on the carrying of an identification pass with a photograph in it. Rather than submit to this regulation most squatters returned to the Reserves, abandoning their homes and most of their stock.

Since earliest times the Kikuyu had lived in scattered groups of huts over the whole of

59

the land, each family living on its own territory. Villages were no more than a shop, school, bus stop and Native Authority Courthouse and meeting place. During the emergency this scattering of the whole population made control extremely difficult, so new villages were built within stockades and all the people were gathered into these areas so that curfew regulations could be enforced and, it must be stressed, so that they could be the more easily defended against Mau Mau attack. Not only were the Kikuyu huts scattered, the holdings of a family might be fragmented in small fields and strips that were often two or three miles apart. Even before the emergency a start had been made in certain areas on consolidating holdings (most notably in the South Tetu location under Chief Muhoya). With the gathering of the Kikuyu into villages the opportunity to consolidate the holdings became easier. Fragmented holdings were pooled, and in each unit the farmer received a new grant of land in one or two parcels. Thus out of this period came eventually as great an agricultural advance as a political one.

With the consolidation of his holdings the Kikuyu farmer obtained a title to his land that could be used as security for a loan to develop his holdings. Restrictions on the planting of 'European' crops such as tea and coffee were lifted and he had at last the chance to practise a balanced farming that gave him cash crops as well as food. In twelve years the Reserves have been transformed from areas of hopeless subsistence agriculture into first-class farmland. Now the African farmer is spreading outwards into the old European areas. Large farms are being bought and converted into smaller units suitable for the new pattern of agriculture.

The Wakamba settled in the Mua hills and on the plains around them. Although of the same basic stock as the Kikuyu, their environment imposed on them a different development. Their territory lies between the highland forests and the *Nyika*, the semi-desert that stretches to the coastal plains. The Wakamba therefore became primarily stock raisers, grazing sheep, cattle and goats on the plains and living in the hills where they grew their foodstuffs. As the plains were full of game they developed into skilful hunters; and as their neighbours, the Masai, coveted their cattle they became warriors whose bravery and ferocity were legendary. These qualities led them to serve with the Army and Police. For many years they were the backbone of these services providing over sixty per cent of their total force, with many more applicants for recruitment than there were places available.

The Wakamba did not increase in numbers as spectacularly as the Kikuyu, but by 1940 their tribal areas were some of the poorest in the country. Overgrazing had reduced vast areas of grassland to bare earth and sheet erosion during the rains had swept away all the valuable topsoil. In the hills overcropping and unthinking digging had had the same effect; deep erosion gullies cut into the earth and as the land got barer and barer the heavy rains had nothing to hold them in the soil. The run-off approached eighty-five per cent of the rain that fell, and millions of tons of soil were carried away each year. At that time it was thought that the Akamba Land Unit was overpopulated and that many Wakamba would have to move to new areas, but in the next twenty years a change described as 'the greatest miracle in Africa' took place. With the devoted and painstaking assistance of Agricultural Officers the Wakamba have learnt to manage their land instead of destroying it. Controlled grazing and enclosure have allowed the grass to grow again, terracing and

60

contour planting have checked the erosion of the hillsides, afforestation of the hilltops has checked the run-off, small dams have impounded water that previously ran to waste so that cattle do not have to trek miles, destroying the vegetation cover by their passage. Instead of there being insufficient land, it was found that progress was being held up for the lack of families to develop the land that had been reclaimed.

The Wakamba families that once scratched a bare subsistence from the scanty soil now graze their cattle on managed grasslands that support a beast per acre. They grow cash crops of tea, coffee and pineapples and run a thriving market-garden industry that supplies Nairobi with vegetables, strawberries and citrus fruit. It is an achievement of which all who contributed can feel justifiably proud.

38   Coffee-picking on a Kikuyu farm

# 5 The Pastoralists

BETWEEN THE UPLAND DWELLERS of Kenya and north-eastern Tanganyika and the lacustrine peoples of the west is a great wedge of semi-nomadic tribes who live a pastoral life, grazing vast herds on the grasslands of the Rift Valley and the Central Plains. They are all of Nilo-Hamitic stock, springing from common ancestors who spread into Africa from south-east Africa (see fig. 8). Some of these Hamites (Boran, Rendille and Galla) settled in Ethiopia and Somaliland, others trekked into the Nile Valley and mixed with the Nilotics. Then they pushed southwards, driving their cattle with them until they arrived in the savannah of East Africa. Here they settled, spreading over the land, fighting the Bushmen who were the only occupiers of the grassveld. Being cattle owners, they were not interested in the forests of the highlands or the fertile farmlands of the lake shores, so an equilibrium was soon established between themselves and their neighbours. There was constant raiding and warfare along the borders, but no real extension of territory.

In the years that have elapsed since the fusion of the two races, variations have taken place resulting in the evolution of many different, though still related, tribes. They have a common basic culture and many still speak forms of the same language but their most striking feature is their physical appearance. They are a tall slender people with fine cut faces and high cheek bones. Their noses are thin, often aquiline, and their lips are not everted like the Bantu. Constantly in movement over their huge territories, they can cover enormous distances with little fatigue. Their lives are lived in isolation, insulated from many of the changes taking place around them.

In addition to their physical similarity, the pastoral tribes have a common culture based upon their cattle. Just as they show their non-Bantu origin in the fineness of their features, their cattle show their descent from the humped and wide-horned cattle of Asia that came into the Nile Valley with the original Hamites and which then came south. To a Masai, a Turkana, a Karamojong, the whole of his life is centred on his cattle. Their needs of water and grass control his daily movements and his annual migrations from dry-weather areas to wet-weather grazing. His wealth is assessed by the number of cattle he owns. Within this common culture there is a wide variation in the status of cattle in the tribal life.

The two extremes are shown by the Turkana and the Masai. To the Turkana cattle are objects of veneration. In his herd will be several animals that he looks on as special intermediaries between himself and his ancestors. They are treated as sacred and are told all the news of the day. At dances and during festivals they are sung to. The mystical devotion of the Turkana to his animals is in direct contrast to the practical thinking of the Masai to whom his animals are wealth. Not wealth in terms of the money they represent as beef, but units of wealth. The Masai point of view can be best understood from a conversation that took place during an attempt by a District Commissioner to get the local Masai to agree to cull

39   The Masai country, looking from the Ngong Hills across the
Rift Valley

their cattle and thus improve them. The D.C. had explained at great length how reducing the herd would make more grazing available to the remaining cattle which would then become fatter and be worth much more. The Masai elder searched for a time in his pouch, then held out a twenty-shilling note in each hand. One note dirty, torn, creased; the other new. 'These are like my cattle,' he said. 'Which note is worth more? Which note will buy me more in the shop?'

All the pastoral peoples are inveterate cattle thieves, reiving far across their borders. The Masai have a theological justification for this, as they believe that in the beginning, when Engai created the world, he gave all the cattle to the Masai, therefore any cattle now owned by others must have been at some time stolen from the Masai and it is perfectly proper to take these errant animals back into custody. The much more prosaic sociological reason for the incessant cattle raiding is the necessity for a young man to accumulate a sufficient herd of cattle with which to buy wives when he becomes an elder.

Although only one of the tribes that make up the group of Nilo-Hamitic pastoralists, the Masai became the best known, as it was through their territory that the main routes into the interior passed. At the time that the first journeys to the inland lakes were being made, the Masai were still probing southwards across the great Central Plains, and it was not until the middle of the nineteenth century that the expansion was stopped by the Wahehe who held the highlands round Iringa. The vast territory they roamed gave early travellers the idea that they were a numerous people who controlled a great kingdom, but in fact the Masai were never very many nor was there any form of central government of their territory.

40  A Masai woman draws water from a water-hole. The containers are made from dried gourds

They were organised in a loose clan and sub-clan system based on age-sets of youth, warrior and elder, the unit of settlement being the *manyatta*, a camp of varying degrees of permanence.

From his earliest days the Masai child is brought up with cattle; as soon as he can toddle he herds goats, as he grows older he moves to a calf herd, trekking with it to and from the waterhole. In his teens he is raised to the grade of *moran* or warrior together with the rest of his age-set. He then leaves his home *manyatta* and sets up a separate one with the others of his grade. He takes with him some cattle so that the *manyatta* will be provided with the basic necessities, and with the warriors go the girls of the age-set to look after the domestic affairs of the *manyatta* and to act as communal concubines.

The time that he is a *moran* is the high point of a Masai's life, for it is the warriors who have pride of place in the tribal hierarchy. In the old days they raided across the length and breadth of the land, their war parties fell on Mombasa and the coastal strip, the rich lands of the Kavirondo Gulf of Lake Victoria, the grasslands of the north around Baringo and the hill country of Southern Tanganyika; they penetrated the forest barrier of the Kikuyu and hunted them along the mountain ridges; they fought long and bloody battles with the Wakamba, the Luo and the Kisii. But however deep their warriors penetrated into other tribal areas, the Masai never extended their territory, they were not interested in more land

64

as long as they had room for their herds. After a raid they carried back the captured cattle and women to their own land and enjoyed the fruits of their victory.

When not raiding, the *moran* divided his time between hunting lion for sport, feasting, dancing and dandifying himself. With his body smeared with red ochre from special pits, his hair intricately plaited and smoothed into a helmet with a mixture of ochre and cow dung, his shield of hide painted with a pattern of red, white and black, his spears (the wooden-hafted stalking spear with a short blade and the long iron throwing spear with the three-foot blade honed to a razor edge) in his hand, his short sword in a red scabbard at the waist, copper ornaments in his ears, silver, copper and pure tin bracelets on his arms, the Masai is a figure of savage beauty and great power. Stonily indifferent to the outside world, he is utterly contemptuous of anyone not fortunate enough to be a Masai. It is no wonder that the first travellers idolised this tribe, so that the legends grew round them until they had the same aura as the Indians of America and their life became idealised as an Arcadian existence harking back to some primeval golden age of man.

After his years of glory, the *moran* is elevated with the rest of his age-set to the status of elder. The *manyatta* is dissolved, he takes his herd of cattle, swollen by raids and natural increase, buys himself a wife (quite often exogamously from the neighbouring Kikuyu, Chagga or Arusha) and settles down to an old age of complete idleness supported by his women and his cattle. As an elder he is respected and takes part in discussions to arrange local matters, but there has never been one chief who is acknowledged as the tribal head. The nearest that the Masai have to a paramount leader is the office of *Laibon*, which is held by a man respected for his magical powers – a spiritual leader rather akin to the Dalai Lama of Tibet, with no temporal powers at all.

Of all the peoples of East Africa, the Masai resisted change for the longest period, and even now much of their way of life is little altered. Their staple diet is still a mixture of blood (drawn from the vein in the neck of a cow) mixed with milk. They still roam the great Central Plains; their warriors, unable now to show their manhood by constant raiding, still show it by hunting lion on foot with nothing but a spear. The traditional method is for a group to surround a lion in open country, forming a large circle round it. Gradually the

41  Modern machinery harvests
the crop of a farmer in
the Rift Valley

65

circle is closed, the warriors moving slowly inwards. The lion, at first curious, gets more and more agitated. He stands at bay, tail switching from side to side in anger. The circle closes silently, step by step. The lion makes a series of short charges stopping always before reaching the line of spears. The circle closes tighter. The lion crouches, gathering his muscles for a charge to destroy the ring which is tightening around him. At last he breaks, leaping forwards, his legs driving him at one person in the ring. The *moran* stands unflinching, the butt of his great spear grounded to take the shock of the lion's charge. As the lion springs he raises the spear to transfix the beast; only when he has done so, standing his ground, will the others crowd in to finish off the kill.

Since the turn of the century pressures, both internal and external, have been building up to force change on the Masai. First there was the splitting of the tribe when Lenana and Sendeyo, the sons of the great *Laibon* Mbatian, went to war with each other over the succession. Sendeyo took the southern half of the land, Lenana the portion that now lies in Kenya. With the coming of the European, the lands were reduced as large portions were alienated for settlement. The finest grazing, 100,000 acres in the Rift Valley, were given to Lord Delamere. Further alienations then cut off the Laikipia Masai from the main body of the tribe and a special corridor a mile wide had to be left to allow cattle to be moved between the two areas. After some time the corridor was closed by the Government. Finally, as the rich grazing land of Laikipia was wanted for the settlement of Europeans, the whole of the Masai in that area were moved into the Rift Valley section of their land, despite the protests of the elders and the attempt of their *Laibon* Legalishu to challenge the decision in the courts.

The contraction of the Masai grazing areas has been matched by an increase in the numbers of their cattle due to better veterinary services, so that the tradition of unlimited grazing of the grasslands has become impossible. Huge areas were becoming impoverished and the grass cover eaten bare. Attempts to reduce the stock of the Masai and to get them to manage their grasslands were bitterly resisted for many years, but since 1955 several schemes have been started and a fine lead has been given by the Reverend Daudi Mokinyu, a Masai who runs his own ranch in the Kajiado area. But progress is very slow and there is still little desire to sell cattle as slaughter stock for money.

If the Masai have made the least change in their life, it is certain that the Kipsigis have altered the most. They are part of a large sub-group of the Nilo-Hamites who are called Kalenjin after the language that they have in common. This group includes the Nandi, Elgeyo, Suk, Tugen, Kamasia and many smaller tribes in addition to the Kipsigis. They spread into Kenya from Mount Elgon and live in an arc to the north-west of the Masai on the hills between the Mau escarpment of the Rift Valley and the lake tribes of the Kisii and the Luo. To occupy this land they drove out a legendary tribe known to them as the Sirikwa, a people who lived in shallow circular depressions in the ground roofed over with poles and turfs. Remains of these dwellings are dotted all over the Sotik hills.

The Kipsigis started as pure pastoralists, but by the beginning of this century were planting maize and millet in small quantities. After the 1914–18 war there was a considerable settlement of Europeans in the Kericho area, and several mission stations were established – notably one at Litein. The great breakthrough came with the introduction of an

44  The irrepressible grin of
    the Gogo

45  Chepkwoin arap Kalya,
    a Kipsigi near Litein

ox-drawn plough. Previously cultivation had been by hoe, traditional women's work, but the plough needed oxen and ox driving was man's work, so the whole cultivation was taken over by men. In addition to this the Kipsigis were willing to be taught agriculture, they did not disdain it as unmanly; from the first they learnt to contour-plough their steep fields and took a pride in the skilful driving this form of ploughing requires. They enclosed their land, dividing it into fields separated by cattle-proof hedges of Mauritius thorn or *Euphorbia*. They learned to manage these fields as part of a mixed farm economy and diversified their crops, planting tea and pyrethrum for cash; wattle for timber and as a cash crop for the tan bark. To the south their lands run out into the bush and pasture of the Sotik and Chepalungu, an area held as commonage, where the surplus stock from the farms is sent to graze. Increases of stock above the holding ability of the land are sold for beef without hesitation. Today the Kipsigis' areas look like a well-tended part of England with neat hedges, green fields of grass with grazing cattle alternating with fields of maize, each farm with a well-thatched and whitewashed set of huts and barns: a model of good farming management.

Between the development extremes of the Kipsigis and the Masai lie the other pastoral peoples. The Nandi, the Elegeyo, Tugen and Njemps have followed the lead given by the Kipsigis. They are learning new farming methods and attaining great skill in the management of irrigation schemes. The Turkana, Karamojong and Suk inhabit the dry grass plains to the north of Mount Elgon, remaining purely pastoral, raiding each other's cattle incessantly. In the dry semi-desert round the Matthews Range live the Samburu, whose nomadic life is epitomised in their name – a corruption of the Masai word for butterfly.

From the shores of Lake Victoria in north-western Tanganyika to the southern highlands there live a group of tribes who practise a mixed agriculture of crop cultivation and cattle raising. All these tribes are of Bantu stock, but in some there has been an Hamitic intrusion, and one, the Wagogo, has been influenced deeply by the Masai. To all these peoples cattle are an important part of the economy but that is all. Nowhere is there the reverence for the cow found in the Nilo-Hamitic pastoralists; to them cattle are food or an investment showing a high return.

The earliest records of travellers in Central Africa speak of the Gogo, for their land lies across the main route to the lakes and all the caravans had to pass through it. Burton called it the 'Burning, fiery plain' and went on to compare the surface of the land to 'a well-metalled road or an untidy expanse of gravel walk' and it must be confessed that at the height of the dry season this is not an unjust comparison. After the rains, however, the apparently arid soil bursts into bloom, grass appears as if by magic from what looked like red concrete, hundreds of species of flowers bloom briefly and the thorn bushes are soft with delicate green leaves. To the west of the Gogo Plain is the equally daunting 'Itigi Thicket', Burton's 'Mgunda Mkali', an area of 2,000 square miles (about the size of Leicestershire) of dense, almost impenetrable, scrub and thorn bush, growing to fifteen feet in height; the haunt of rhinoceros and Greater Kudu.

The early traveller in this inhospitable country was further troubled by the incessant demands for *hongo* (tribute) from the Gogo chiefs through whose territory he passed. The Wagogo have never had any great sense of tribal cohesion and they are organised in a large number of petty divisions of clan relationships. Thus each 'chief' controlled only a very small area and no sooner had one paid an outrageous tribute and been allowed to pass on, than one was in another chief's area and had to satisfy yet another swingeing demand for *hongo*. The chiefs developed this extortion of tribute to a very high skill. They had to get the largest amount of tribute they could without turning the caravans away as they needed to keep trade with the Coast alive to enable them to maintain a market for their ivory, of which they had an abundance.

In the 1880s the Gogo were over-run by the Masai. They left their imprint on the Gogo, who adopted their red ochre hairdressing, red dyed body and red blanket. This imitation was most probably an attempt to attach to themselves some of the frightening aura of the Masai but they never achieved the pride or stony insolence of the true Masai. Perhaps this is because cheerfulness will keep breaking in, for when not going about the serious business of extortion (avarice is a passion with them) the Gogo is perennially cheerful. He is also the traditional buffoon and butt. In any African story about the outwitting of a simpleton or a lack of sophistication it is usually a Gogo who is named as the typical example. In addition to their cheerfulness they also have a very high musical ability; most of them carry a small instrument made of a resonating box with steel prongs of different lengths which they pluck to produce a very pleasant twanging noise. Hugh Tracy, the authority on African music, has written that their singing and drumming is some of the best that he has recorded in all Africa.

This cheerfulness is all the more surprising when one thinks of the hardness of their life. Their land is of very low fertility, in some areas very badly eroded and subject to disastrous droughts. In 1953–4 there was a severe famine caused by the failure of the rains and it is estimated that three-quarters of the domestic livestock of the tribe was sold, eaten, or died of starvation during this time. Their agriculture, which has a staple of millet, sorghum and maize, is marginal in that it needs rainfall slightly above the average to be expected over a number of years to bring the crops to fruition. As Ugogo lies in a 'rain shadow' area, the fluctuations of yearly rainfall are great and famines are almost endemic. The answer would seem to be to try to change the staple food to one more suited to the rainfall (such as cassava) but the Gogo are a stubborn and conservative people and a radical alteration in their diet seems to be unlikely.

To the north of the Gogo live two related tribes, the Wanyemwezi and the Wasukuma, of Bantu stock with a certain amount of Hamitic infiltration, particularly amongst the Sukuma. The name Wanyemwezi means 'the people of the country of the moon' and early travellers hearing this linked the name with the old tradition of the 'Mountains of the Moon' but in actual fact the name was given to them by the coastal Swahili as a description that they came from the far west – the land where the new moon was first seen. They gained early fame for their ability as porters and quickly established a virtual monopoly of the carriage of trade goods and ivory for the Arab caravans. They also became slavers, preying on the neighbouring tribes and trading their captives for rifles and powder. They were a people of small chieftains, each for himself only, until the coming of Mirambo. Stanley christened him the 'Napoleon of Central Africa' and it is a not inapt comparison.

Mirambo started as a typical small chief but soon built up a reputation as a mercenary, hiring himself and his picked band of warriors to other chiefs who needed any fighting done.

46   The snake dance of the Wasukuma

He slowly gathered an army round him large enough to take over other chiefdoms. This conquest placed him astride the main Arab trade routes to the lakes and he demanded tribute from all the caravans that passed. Mirambo was not against the Arabs, indeed he wanted their caravans to continue passing through his territory, but he was insistent on their having to pay for the protection he would give them. The Arabs were unwilling to pay, so a war developed which effectively paralysed trade for some years. Mirambo's army was exceedingly well trained and he could muster about 7,000 warriors of whom 500 were his *corps d'élite* which he always led in person. Most of the warriors were armed with muzzle-loaders but Mirambo also acquired some modern breech-loading rifles and this gave him a useful advantage in most of the fights he undertook. The Arabs found him a very different foe from the usual African villagers they raided for slaves and the war was a bloody affair of many engagements fought with great ferocity. Eventually it was the Arabs who had to capitulate and make terms. They never forgot and spoke of Mirambo in bitter tones, making him out a cruel and bloodthirsty monster; mostly, one suspects, to bolster their own self-esteem after being defeated.

The early explorers who met Mirambo grew to like and respect him and found that he really wanted to give his empire the benefit of trade with the outside world. He tried very hard to persuade the Church Missionary Society to come to his land instead of going to Buganda and was disappointed when they refused. Later he helped the London Missionary Society to settle in his area, not because of any religious conversion but hoping that the

70

knowledge that missionaries were safely settled would encourage traders to overcome their fear of him. Although Sir John Kirk never met him personally he was most impressed with the reports he had of Mirambo, and at one time considered entering into treaty with him. The tragedy was that on Mirambo's death in 1884 the empire he had built crumbled away into the fragments of petty chiefdoms from which he had built it up. He left no one capable of consolidating his work.

Usukuma means 'the land to the north' and this descriptive name has been attached to the tribe that inhabited the land to the north of the Wanyemwezi rather than the more usual way of the tribe giving their name to the land on which they settle. The first inhabitants of Sukumaland were hunters rather than agriculturalists and they therefore chose to settle in the lush areas of the west rather than the grassy plains to the east. They were Bantu spreading out from the Congo forests and banding together in small groups with no tribal organisation. Each group cleared its own patch of bushland under an elected leader called a *Batemi* (or 'Chief Cutter'). At about the same time a group of Hamitic origin also entered Sukumaland. They were of the usual tall, fine-boned Hamitic structure and were accepted quite naturally by the Bantu as their leaders. Having no clan connections these Hamites could dispense justice impartially and they were undoubtedly superior to the Bantu both physically and mentally. They brought with them their knowledge of cattle-keeping and taught their subjects the art. From this amalgam the present Wasukuma have grown. Though they are still a people of small individual chiefdoms, each chief proudly traces his lineage back to some splendid but mythical Hamitic leader.

The first settlements were built under the huge granite tors that dot the land. They were hedged with a *Euphorbia* which when cut, exudes a thick milky sap that causes intense pain, even blindness, if it gets in the eyes. When the Germans came much of the internecine fighting ceased and the Sukuma expanded, settling farther and farther away from the old centres.

The spreading of the tribe over the land soon brought the usual problems of overstocking and erosion. The country itself is open with a thin cover of grass over poor rocky soil. Scattered over the land are occasional masses of rock piled up in heaps of giant boulders.

47  The bare plain of Usukuma dominated by a lonely baobab tree

The bareness of the landscape is accentuated by the lack of trees. The Sukuma have a hatred for trees and cut them down as quickly as possible, believing that the trees, by providing perching places, attract the birds that steal their seeds and crops. The only trees for mile after mile are the massive baobabs, grotesque trees with monstrous grey trunks and puny-looking branches. The Kikuyu of Kenya believe them to have been planted upside down by God when he was angry. They say that what sticks up above the ground is the old root system of the tree and that the real branches are underground – an acute observation, for the roots really are huge and branching. They adduce as proof of this dogma the fact that you never see a sapling baobab; they are always massive and full-grown, and this must obviously be so for it would be impossible for a tree actually to start growing upside down; it must start right way up and is only turned over when well grown. Despite its ugly shape the baobab has many uses. The fruit is encased in a large gourd which when dried makes an excellent receptacle for milk or water; the flesh is a tart white substance that draws the mouth and is most refreshing in the heat; the tree itself often has cavities in the trunk that hold water in times of drought, and nearly every tree has a swarm of bees in a smaller hole in the trunk or branches. The Sukuma drive a ladder of wooden pegs into the soft bark of the tree to help them to collect the honey and the wax, the sale of which provides welcome cash in their economy.

The Sukuma were used as a test-bed for some of the early attempts to implement the policy of 'indirect rule'. The theory was that the multitude of petty chiefs were to be federated into one paramount chiefdom and control over the whole country was to be exercised by a council elected from the chiefs. This Sukumaland Federation was only partly successful, for although it succeeded in amalgamating all the local native treasuries into one Federal treasury, individual chiefs were too jealous of their powers to surrender these to a central council. The Federation did, however, have powers as a court of appeal from local tribunals and the pooling of the treasuries allowed the Sukumaland Development Scheme to work.

The Sukumaland Development Scheme was basically a scheme of self-help to rehabilitate the areas that were over-populated and to open up new areas that were waterless and tsetse-fly-infested. By constructing dams and hafirs in the dry areas settlers were attracted. They then cleared the bush by the communal co-operative labour that is a tradition of the Wasukuma, a relic of the turbulent past when to work by oneself in the open was to court death or enslavement. The clearings destroyed the habitat of the fly, cattle could be kept and pastures were built up by controlled grazing. The scheme entailed a great deal of very hard work and co-operation, both of which were forthcoming from the industrious Sukuma, who now are one of the largest cattle-producers in Tanzania as well as providing much of the country's cotton for export.

Sukumaland is also the site of another form of riches for it was at Mwadui in 1940 that Dr Williamson found the world's largest diamond mine. The story of the strike is legendary and like most legends it has produced a goodly crop of myths. Williamson was a Canadian, and originally came to Tanganyika as a prospector for de Beers. He became convinced that the area round Shinyanga contained a big 'pipe' of diamonds. When his first searches proved fruitless he was recalled by de Beers, but he resigned, so strong was his conviction

48  Two Haya with their gourds of beer pause for a roadside chat

that he was right. He continued to prospect the area on his own, for a long time without any success. His funds ran out and he was dependent on a 'grub stake' by a local Indian store owner. Living barely above subsistence level on maize meal, his gear carried on a donkey, he finally triumphed, finding signs of the 'pipe' under a baobab near Shinyanga. It was not a lucky or opportunist find but the result of complete professional conviction and the hard unremitting application of all his geological training. It was a triumph of dedication and expertise that succeeded where many had failed; for there had been many other prospectors in the same area. There is a story (perhaps one of the myths of this strike) that a geologist from the Government once made his headquarters on top of the Mwadui pipe and that in the excavation for his lavatory pit were subsequently found some large diamonds. The mine for many years contributed to the economy by the payment of a royalty to the Government and now it is owned by the Government of Tanzania in partnership with de Beers.

North-west and west of Usukuma are a group of tribes that are related to the Sukuma and the Wanyemwezi, but which have a much larger proportion of Hamitic infiltration. The Haya now live on the shores of Lake Victoria, but originally they came from near

Bunyoro in Uganda, a region they left because of the ceaseless wars. Their land is extremely fertile and they grow bananas and sweet potatoes as their staple food crops. They make a beer from the bananas which is drunk at all times, even when walking or riding from place to place. The traveller sucks the brew through a straw from a gourd, never having to pause in his journey except to replenish his gourd. Coffee has been grown in the area for over three hundred years and recently the Haya have taken up cotton growing as a second cash crop. Their prosperity has had a most unfortunate effect, for the long weeks of idleness with no work to do except wait for the various harvests are spent in vacant beer-swilling by the men who live in a state of almost permanent inebriation and disease. This unsatisfactory home life drives many Buhaya women to the large towns where they are notorious as prostitutes.

South of Ugogo the land rises into a country of rolling ridges, deep river valleys and high mountains, the home of the Hehe, a tribe famous for its warriors and the prolonged fight it made against the Germans. Although one of the larger tribes of Tanganyika, the Hehe are really thirty or so small tribes that have welded themselves into one. The consolidation of the tribe was achieved by two remarkable chiefs, Muyugamba and his son Mkwawa. About 1850 Muyugamba, who was a small chief of the Muyinga clan, started to extend his authority by conquest; the more he conquered the more powerful and irresistible he became and by the time of his death in about 1880 he had established a hegemony over the majority of the tribes who make up the Hehe. On his death his son Mkwawa was driven away by rival claimants to the chiefdom, but returned in two years and started to extend his father's conquests. In 1882–3 he inflicted crushing defeats on the Ngoni and the Wanyemwezi, his two warlike neighbours. The Hehe then fought the Gogo and established control over the whole of Southern Tanganyika from the Portuguese border to Kilosa. The only challenge to this was the Masai who over-ran the Gogo, but they were finally defeated in a battle in which the Hehe were led by Mkwawa's sister, one of his most trusted sub-chiefs.

As the German caravans started their penetrations of the interior, Mkwawa levied a heavy toll from them, ambushing and killing any that tried to slip through his country without paying. He was implacably opposed to the Germans and allied himself to Bushiri during his revolt. In 1891 the Germans decided to send an expedition against Mkwawa. He ambushed the column in the Katinga Valley and all but annihilated it, capturing over three hundred rifles, field guns and plenty of ammunition. Mkwawa then continued his raiding and built himself an extremely strong base at Kalenga (near the modern Iringa). The Germans sent another force against him in 1894. They attacked Kalenga with cannons, and after a long shelling, breached the defences. This did not end the battle, for the Hehe fought savagely for every hut and in the hand-to-hand struggle Mkwawa managed to escape. From this time on the Germans hunted him relentlessly but Mkwawa continued to elude them, the Hehe giving him unswerving loyalty, supplying him with food and information, helping his warriors and sacrificing themselves rather than let him be captured. In 1898 the Germans offered a reward of 5,000 rupees (a fantastic sum at that time) for his head and this at last tempted someone to betray his whereabouts. A Sergeant-Major Merkl was sent to capture him but when he came upon Mkwawa and his companion he found they were already dead, Mkwawa having taken his own life rather than be captured. Merkl cut off his head, which was sent back to Germany, his body being given to the Hehe for burial.

Mkwawa remained a hero to his people after his death and his family rule the Hehe to this day. The tribe made many and repeated attempts to get the head of their chief returned to them; the very first request made to the British Administrator who took over Iringa after it was captured during the 1914–18 war was for the head to be returned. A special clause was included in the Treaty of Versailles requiring the return of the skull from Germany, but nothing was done until 1954, when, as a result of a personal visit by the Governor (Sir Edward Twining) to the museum concerned, the skull was retrieved and brought to Uhehe where it was ceremonially handed over by the Governor to Chief Adam Sapi, grandson of Mkwawa and the chief of the Hehe.

Today the Hehe live in one of the most attractive parts of the country, a rolling plateau that varies between 4,000 and 6,500 feet in height and is too high for tsetse fly. Their staple crop is maize, with millet and rice in the lower areas and subsidiary crops of just about anything that grows. Iringa, the main township, has been the centre of European settlement and there are many farms round it producing tobacco. In the savannah lands of the Southern Highlands a settlement scheme was started by Lord Chesham, but this has not proved wholly successful as the soil was found to be deficient in many respects. At Mufindi and Lupembe there are large tea estates and pyrethrum and coffee are also produced in the area. Travelling along the roads that give wonderful panoramic views over the grasslands and hills it is difficult to reconcile this peaceful beauty with the long years of bloodshed. The country is now fertile, lush with growth, the atmosphere always soft with moisture, for there are rivers everywhere and the dry plains of Ugogo and Unyemwezi are like a dream.

# 6 The Peoples of the Lakes

OF ALL THE REGIONS OF EAST AFRICA, Uganda is the most densely populated and the one that gives the greatest sense of an ordered and stable civilisation. The density of population is due to the fertility of the soil helped by an abundant rainfall, and the stability goes back before the coming of the Europeans to the African Kingdoms which themselves hark back to the 'Sudanic' Kingdoms of the first centuries A.D.

Except in the north-east where the land merges into the dry semi-deserts of Kenya's Northern Frontier District, Uganda is a land of lakes and rivers. Over one-seventh of its surface is covered in water. As it also lies across the equator there is a constant cycle of evaporation from the lakes and precipitation as rain when the moisture-laden air meets the dry winds that blow from the plains of Kenya and Tanganyika. Plentiful rainfall on a fertile soil has given the country a range of crops that has ensured prosperity and freedom from hunger for many generations and this has in turn encouraged the formation of stable societies. Because of this, Uganda suffered very little from the depredations of the slave trade. The strong kings with well-organised armies and the dense population that could rally immediately in the event of danger made the normal slave trader's tactics of surprise swoops on poorly defended villages useless. There was, therefore, very little loss of men to slavers during the last century and although there was constant warfare between the kingdoms, the losses were sustainable and did not seriously affect the growth of the populations.

Because of the structure of the kingdoms, the pattern of society in Uganda is very different from that in other territories. When one refers to the Kikuyu or the Gogo one is talking about a single ethnic group, with a common origin and a homogeneous composition, but when one talks of the Ankole or the Baganda one is talking about a society that has several quite distinct groups in it. There is, of course, a certain amount of intermixing in the middle, but the ruling class are usually pure-blooded Nilotics and the peasants are Bantu.

There are three main groups of Africans in Uganda and they are separated from each other by well-defined geographical features. Across the south of the country live the Bantu, completely surrounded by lakes and rivers, from the shores of Lake Victoria northwards to the long fingers of Lake Kyoga, then westwards with the Nile as boundary to Lake Albert and then southwards with the Semliki River as boundary to Lake Edward. To anthropologists this group is known as the inter-lacustrine Bantu and it is here, between the lakes, that the kingdoms of Uganda grew, fought with each other and flourished. North of Lake Kyoga and westwards to the Albert Nile live the Nilotics, with the Sudanic Madi and Lugbara on the west bank. To the east, where the Karamoji Hills mark the division, are the Nilo-Hamitic pastoralists who spread into Kenya.

The actual period of the Nilotic incursion into the Bantu area is not known with any exactitude, and attempts to date it are complicated by the constant allusions in tribal legends

76

49   Fishing boats setting out across Lake Victoria

to another people referred to as the Bachwezi. Throughout the area there are large earthworks, some obviously defensive, some religious. These are thought to have been made by the people called Bachwezi who are remembered in stories as tall men, with straight red hair. They were a powerful people, with a complete command of magic and witchcraft and an ability to work metals. They are still mentioned with awe and sites at which they are known to have worshipped are still places of reverence. Persistence of legend is usually a good guide to actuality and where excavations have been carried out the earthworks have yielded late Iron-Age implements. There is a striking similarity between the plan of the earthworks at Bigo and the ruins at Zimbabwe in Southern Africa, also built by a 'lost' civilisation. The explanation that is now most generally accepted is that the Bachwezi were the descendants of the ancient Sudanic civilisation of Meroë. On the collapse of this civilisation in the fourth century A.D. the culture moved eastwards to Kordofan, then south to Lake Chad, finally coming back to the Southern Sudan. It is possible that the Bachwezi were of this culture, continuing their wanderings southward. It is interesting that the name is still used by a secret society (akin to freemasons) which flourishes amongst the Ha of Western Tanganyika.

The Bahima came from the north about five hundred years ago, probably from the same stock as the Bachwezi. They were a powerful people who built fairly large towns. One set of earthworks in Ankole encloses a town of about a quarter of a mile square dominated by a U-shaped fort. It was the Bahima who brought with them the huge horned cattle that are shown on the old reliefs in the tombs of the Egyptian Pharaohs; the high cheek bones, aquiline noses and thin lips to be seen in the men on these carvings are still duplicated in the features of the modern Bahima. Although they had an influence over the whole of this area and farther south in Tanganyika, the Bahima made their capital in Ankole, absorbing the

77

50 & 51   Ankole cattle, direct descendants of the cattle of the Pharaohs.
The relief is from the British Museum

Bantu of the area into their feudal structure as their peasant cultivators. Ankole is a place ideally suited to these people for it is a stretch of open grassy downland, well watered and fertile, where the Bahima can live their withdrawn and haughty life tending their cattle, leaving the cultivation of the land to the *Bairo*, the original Bantu. One very odd custom of the Bahima was their practice of force-feeding their kings and the brides of their nobles with milk. Travellers at the turn of the century saw many brides so fat that they could only crawl on hands and knees, who had to be carried on litters, sometimes needing eight men to lift them. The late *Omugabe* (King) of Ankole weighed over twenty-six stone and had to be manhandled into his car. Amongst a people of such slim beauty this practice is all the more strange.

It was from the Bahima that the kingdoms of Uganda obtained the doctrine of divine kingship, but it needed a mingling of the Bahima blood with that of the fiercer Nilotic Luo to produce the rulers who established these kingdoms. The greatest of these was Bunyoro-Kitara, which at the height of its power encompassed the whole of Uganda south of the Victoria Nile. In the eighteenth century the kingdom of Buganda was founded by a cadet branch of the Bunyoro dynasty and was for many years a small tributary of the larger empire. Then in the early part of the nineteenth century the eldest son of the *Mukama* (King) seized a portion of the land and carved out for himself the kingdom of Toro at the foot of the Ruwenzori Mountains. From this time onwards the power of Bunyoro diminished whilst Toro and Buganda rose steadily. When Speke journeyed to the source of the Nile he stayed some time at the Court of Kamrasi, the Mukama of Bunyoro-Kitara, and found him an exceedingly unattractive monarch ruling 'a wild set of ragamuffins'. Kamrasi stripped Speke of guns, books, watches, medicines, everything he could extract; he repeated this action two years later when Samuel Baker visited him on the journey during which he discovered Lake Albert. On this occasion Kamrasi nearly got shot when he suggested that in addition to taking nearly all their possessions he should also take Mrs Baker. On this Mrs

Baker, 'with a countenance almost as amiable as the head of Medusa', harangued Kamrasi in Arabic (which he didn't understand) while her husband drew his revolver and resolved to sell her honour dearly. This combined attack overawed Kamrasi and he gave permission for this redoubtable pair to depart. Baker's description ends with this little gem: 'I assisted my wife on to her ox and with a very cold *adieu* to Kamrasi, I turned my back most gladly on the place.'

It was in Buganda that the doctrine of the King's divinity and complete authority was developed to the full. The Kabaka was all powerful, chiefs held from him their lands and wealth, but he could dispossess them at will thus depriving them of the rents and taxes they collected from the peasant cultivators. This complete autocracy is well illustrated in an extract from Speke's Journal, describing an audience with the Kabaka Mutesa in 1858:

> 'The King now loaded one of the carbines I had given him with his own hands, and giving it full cock to a page, told him to go out and shoot a man in the outer court; which was no sooner accomplished than the little urchin returned to announce his success, with a look of glee such as one might see on the face of a boy who had robbed a bird's nest, caught a trout or done any other boyish trick. The King said "Did you do it well?" "Oh yes, capitally." I never heard, and there appeared no curiosity to know, what individual human being the urchin had deprived of life.'

The dominance of the Baganda was finally established by the coming of the Europeans for it was with them that the first treaties were made and although there were the inevitable misunderstandings and set-backs inherent in this form of alliance there is no doubt that the Baganda came well out of the deal. At the same time the Bunyoro were greatly diminished by their long fight against Britain, led by Kamrasi's son, Kabarega. He has gone down in

52    Mount Baker in the Ruwenzori Mountains. In the foreground
         can be seen the strange vegetation of this region

the history books as a bloody tyrant, but this judgement is based to a large extent on the writings of those against whom he was fighting and the bias implied in this viewpoint is usually forgotten. Typical of such judgements is Sir Frederick Jackson's:

'From the first moment of his succeeding his father, Kamrasi, he acquired for himself a reputation for horrible cruelties and cold-blooded butchery of his subjects, that almost rivalled that of his near neighbour Mutesa, and later on Mwanga. From the former he may be distinguished as possessing all the bad qualities, with the addition of the basest treachery, but none of the better ones; and from the latter, by possessing courage and hatred of us that was so irreconcilable that he never once sued for peace, even when hard pressed; and never grovelled when captured.'

This is rather like the definition of a dangerous animal once given by a French hunter: 'Cet animal est très méchant, quand on l'attaque il se défend.' Perhaps the better judgement on this great fighter is Emin Pasha's. 'He made a very favourable impression on me. He gave me the impression of being a thoroughly hospitable and intelligent man. The treatment accorded to me by Kabalega [sic] was never disturbed by a single unfriendly word.'

The administration of Uganda was based on an hierarchy of chiefs and sub-chiefs controlling their own Councils. Elections were held to each of the Councils – the *Miruka* or parish, the *Gombolola* or district and the *Saza* or county. In order to bolster this system Sir Harry Johnston took the old Buganda system of the allocation of land to chiefs and made a new allocation of all the land in Buganda. The land was split between a thousand chiefs named by the Council of Regents who were governing Buganda during the infancy of the Kabaka Daudi Chwa. The unit of size for this division was the square mile, and to a chief's

53   The pattern of 'mailo' cultivation in the densely populated area around Kampala

54   Cotton being brought into market

private estate (which might easily be 20–25 square miles) was added an official estate of 8 square miles for a Saza chief, and *pro rata* for lesser chiefs. A corruption of the English 'mile' to the Luganda equivalent '*mailo*' was used for the lands so granted and freehold title was given to the chiefs over all this *mailo* land. Originally a register of all land transactions was to be kept, but the volume of mutation was such that the register was soon overwhelmed. The conversion of a basically feudal tenure pattern into a freehold tenancy pattern made great hardship for the cultivators, who suddenly found themselves having to pay rents to a superior landlord. There was, of course, the ability to buy land for oneself, but there can be little doubt that the *mailo* distribution created a two-class society: the rich landowner and the poor tenant cultivator. However, the necessity to pay rent was an incentive to look for cash crops and to this extent the prosperity of Uganda perhaps stems indirectly from the *mailo* system of tenure.

Throughout the inter-lake area bananas are the staple food crop, providing the *Matoke* which is the basic diet of all the Bantu. From it also comes beer and by distillation a powerful gin. Maize, vegetables, sheep, goats and even cattle are all additional foodstuffs, while for cash crops the African grows cotton and coffee. Cotton was introduced into Uganda in 1903 when the British Cotton Growers Association sent two and a half tons of seed to the Church Missionary Society in Kampala to distribute to the Baganda. With the seed the Company also sent leaflets printed in Luganda giving full cultivation instructions and the foundation of

Uganda's prosperity was laid. In 1904 fifty-four bales of cotton were shipped from Uganda, and from then on the industry grew until today the export is a third of a million bales. Coffee is an indigenous shrub in Uganda and has been grown from earliest times. The *robusta* species needs none of the careful tending or preparation of *arabica*. The beans are picked, laid out to dry in the sun, and then sold. The price is, of course, not as high as the *arabica* but there is now so much coffee grown in Uganda that it exceeds cotton in terms of export value.

To the north of the Nile live the Acholi, the Lango and the Alur, the Nilotic tribes that moved down from the Sudan. Although they carry on some farming they are mainly a cattle-raising people. Like the other pastoral tribes the Acholi have no hereditary chief, saving their veneration for the rain-makers and living in small family groups. They do, however, have a very strong religion based on a single great creator *Jok*. Samuel Baker called their land 'the Paradise of Africa' and it is a not unfair description of the great swelling down-lands dotted with thorn trees and borassus palms swarming with every kind of game, watered by the River Asswa and its tributaries, rising gradually in the east to the hills that divide the Acholi from the Karamojong. The Acholi are passionate hunters, and in the old days organised large gatherings to surround and kill whole herds of game. They were fierce warriors and form the backbone of the Army and the Police Force. Nowadays they are settling down to farming on a scale above the old subsistence level. The area is very suitable for tobacco growing and many farms are now producing leaf on a contract basis for the East African Tobacco Company, whilst some of the more advanced farmers are now curing the leaf themselves.

Baker's eulogy of Acholi could in fact be applied to the whole of Uganda, which has a lushness and beauty that is totally unlike the rest of East Africa. The beauty is somehow more like the traditional beauty that the European is accustomed to. The soft green hills and lakes of Kigezi do indeed recall the Lake District. It is perhaps the 'roundness' of the landscape that gives Uganda its sense of maturity; the great rockpiles, the jagged peaks, the emptiness of the plains are all absent, as are the dominant reds and yellows of the rest of East Africa. Uganda is a green land and the moist air gives it a lovely softness. There are, of course, sights that still fill one with awe. The view from the Kanaba Gap over the Rift Valley and the Bufumbira Volcanoes is one that can never be described. The Murchison Falls, where the whole of the Nile forces itself through a 19-foot-wide gap in the rock, is one of the wonders of Africa, and the Ruwenzori Mountains permanently hidden in drifts of mist, the way to them lying through forests of rotting trees and festooning moss, are an area of fantasy removed from the usual meaning of landscape. But over all there is a home-liness absent from the other territories. To the European the order of parishes, villages, district centres and main towns is familiar and comprehensible and because of this the land-scape speaks to him in a familiar idiom.

# 7 The Mountain Dwellers of Tanzania

FROM THE EDGE OF THE RIFT VALLEY in Northern Tanzania there runs a chain of mountains. First the volcanic cone of Mt Meru that rises from the dry Masai plains to 15,000 feet, then, to the east, the majestic bulk of Kilimanjaro, its snowy dome resting on dark green forests. From Kilimanjaro the mountains run east of south, the narrow ridge of the Parés climbing to nearly 8,000 feet, then the slab of the Usambaras rising from the Pangani River valley in a great upthrusting escarpment of naked rock. The top of the slab is cut into a network of valleys with forested ridges in between; the land surface lying at about 6,000 feet above sea-level. The slopes of these mountains are the homes of tribes that had some of the first contacts with Europeans, and on Kilimanjaro live a tribe, the Chagga, who are one of the most advanced in the country.

The Chagga are a mixture of Bantu tribes from the plains, mostly Wateita and Wakamba, who began to live on the lower slopes of Kilimanjaro at the beginning of the seventeenth century. The raids of the Masai most probably drove them into the forest areas, where they absorbed the aboriginal Konyingo who lived there. The soil on the mountain was rich volcanic loam and food growing was an easy matter. The early explorers all speak highly of the industriousness of the Chagga. They were one of the first of the African tribes to be described, and as the news of the great snow mountain on the equator drew explorers to East Africa their habits, language and customs were thoroughly investigated. Krapf and Rebmann knew them well and they were also written up by von der Decken and Sir Henry Johnston, both of whom climbed to about 12,000 feet on the mountain. The first ascent of the dome was made by Dr Hans Meyer in 1889 and was an epic of early mountaineering.

55   Kibo, the snowy dome of Kilimanjaro, seen from the plains

56   A Chagga homestead on the slopes of Kilimanjaro. The women
are sorting coffee beans grown on the bushes under the bananas

The rainfall on the slopes of the mountain varies from 40 to 100 inches per year, but
it is not distributed evenly over the year. In order to make the most of the fertility of the soil
during the dry months the Chagga developed a wonderful irrigation system, leading water
from the many mountain streams over long distances to their plots of land. These irrigation
furrows were supremely well engineered, running across spurs and along precipitous slopes,
sometimes banked up to carry them over small declivities, sometimes channelled through
the rock and always at a perfect grade so that the water ran fast enough to provide a sufficient
volume but not so fast that it scoured and damaged the channel. As the furrows run for
some miles, they obviously cross many different plots of land. The 'Furrow-founder' would
organise help to build the furrow from all the people over whose land it ran. In return, they
would all benefit by being able to extract agreed amounts of water on certain days. These
early co-operative efforts laid a very sound basis for tribal cohesion and stood the Chagga
in good stead when they came to tackle modern crops and marketing.

Because of the explorations of the early travellers and the ease with which Kilimanjaro
could be reached from the Coast, it was one of the first areas brought under missionary
influence. The results of this influence were beneficial not only on the spiritual plane but
also in the strictly material sense. The Roman Catholic mission at Kilema introduced
*arabica* coffee plants in 1902–3 and gradually the cultivation of coffee spread amongst the
Chagga. The number of bushes was still fairly small after the First World War, when Major

84

Dundas (later Sir Charles) was posted to take over the district. He immediately saw the possibilities of the crop and started a campaign to convince the Chagga of the advantages of planting their plots with coffee. At first there was quite a lot of resistance, for the Chagga did not want to uproot their staple banana trees, but when it was pointed out to them that the bananas would act as shade for the coffee and that they could grow both bananas and coffee in the same plot they soon saw the advantages that would accrue, and there was a phenomenal increase in the planting of the crop.

There was early opposition by the European settlers to the planting of coffee as they feared that slack cultivation by the Africans would lead to disease and blight that would have serious effects on their own plantations. In order to present a united front and for the more prosaic reasons of economic expediency, the Chagga growers formed a co-operative that was originally called the Kilimanjaro Native Coffee Planters Association; this acted as a central distribution agency for the crop and also represented the Chagga interests against the pressure from the Europeans. In 1933 this association became known as the Kilimanjaro Native Co-operative Union, and the initials K.N.C.U. became a byword for progress, wealth, and modern thinking; they were a power behind the political advancement of the Chagga. This co-operative, the largest in East Africa, was fortunate in that it had the tradition of Chagga co-operation over irrigation furrows to draw on and it soon became a model of the advantages of self-help amongst the Africans. It also had enough power and authority to ensure good cultivation and insisted on the rooting out and burning of all diseased trees. After the last war the Coffee Research Station at Lyamungu developed a strain of heavy-yielding coffee from selected 'mother' trees, and the distribution of the clones of this strain to all the Chagga growers as replacement stock will lead to a quadrupling of the yield.

The wealth that coffee brought to the Chagga was used wisely by them in providing schools, hospitals and community centres for the tribe. Like the Kikuyu, to whom some authorities think the Chagga are related by blood, they had a thirst for education, and again like the Kikuyu, they had a serious overcrowding problem on their land. The pressure was due to the fact that of all the African areas in Tanganyika the Chagga lands were the only ones hemmed in by European farms so that expansion was impossible. In fact the encirclement was not only by Europeans, for on the north there was the large Masai area that stretched up the mountain to Laitokitok. But it was the barrier of farms between the Chagga and the open plains that caused such dissension. There was such a lack of room that cattle were kept in stalls and fed on banana fibre and loads of grass cut by the Chagga women on the plains and laboriously carried up the mountain to their homes. The pressure was relieved after the last war by buying in many of the farms that surrounded the mountains and creating corridors to the plains.

Mt Meru is a small replica of Kilimanjaro but on its slopes there live two very different tribes. The Meru are related to the Chagga and have a similar way of life, but as the climate is drier and their lands lower they grow pyrethrum as a cash crop rather than coffee. The white daisy of this crop is very beautiful when set out in fields, and from the flower is obtained an insecticidal dust that is still in great demand. On the west side of the mountain live the Waarusha, a Nilo-Hamitic people allied to the Masai, who have left their pastoral life to settle down and grow crops. They have always been under the protection of the

Masai, who have tolerated them for their usefulness in providing grain and as a source of brides for their *moran* to buy when they become elders.

The Paré have only been settled in the range of mountains that bear their name for the past two hundred years. They came from Kenya in three waves, the first two leaderless and unorganised, searching for land for their stock as grazing in their home areas became over-stocked. The third wave was composed of Wateita stock calling themselves Wamjema, and they established control over the whole area through their prowess, knowledge of medicines and proficiency at rain-making. The Paré are mainly an agricultural people with maize as their staple crop, for although their hills rise to over 7,000 feet, the main part of their land is dry and does not support crops that need much rainfall.

As one continues southwards down the road from Moshi to Tanga one crosses a dusty plain of thorn scrub, red earth and baobabs until in front of one there stretches for mile after mile a great wall of rock and forest, the western face of the Usambara Mountains. On this side there are no foothills, the range springs cleanly from the flats with great buttresses of grey rock forcing themselves upward into the blue sky. It is an elemental landscape of great power and as one crawls along the road the cliffs and buttresses seem to overhang and press upon one physically. The only gap in the wall occurs at Mombo where there is a steep valley cutting into the mountain mass. From Mombo the Germans engineered a road that climbs up the side of deep valleys, inches past solid rock faces and crosses waterfalls until it reaches Lushoto, a small town that still has the feeling of some remote village in the Bavarian Alps. There are grassy commons on which goats and sheep graze, wooden chalets tucked into the forest, bright with flowers and countless streams twinkling in the sunlight. In the evenings the air is cold and there is the smell of burning logs and a blue haze of smoke hangs in the valleys.

The Wasambaa first appeared as a unified tribe in the eighteenth century, when a chief called Bega gained control of them but it was his great-grandson, Kimweri, who took the tribe to its greatest heights. In a series of wars of conquest he subjugated the other tribes from Kilimanjaro to the Coast, and was only prevented from extending his empire to the south by the Zigua around Bagamoyo who were armed by their Arab allies with modern firearms. For a long time Kimweri was so powerful that the Sultan of Zanzibar agreed to a joint rule over Tanga, the Governor appointed being answerable to both Kimweri and the Sultan. Krapf became a great friend of Kimweri and was keen to start a mission in Usambara, but it was Abingdon of the Universities Mission to Central Africa who actually founded a station there after meeting Kimweri in 1867.

As in Uchagga and Buganda contact with missionaries brought benefits to the African. Coffee was introduced into Usambara and help was given to the Wasambaa in general agricultural science. This help was increased when the German Government made Amani (in the hills above Muheza) their research centre for tropical agriculture. Many different crops were tried, rubber and cinchona being two of the more successful experiments. Nowadays the Wasambaa practise a mixed farming that includes a certain amount of stock raising, the cultivation of maize and bananas, and cash crops of coffee, wattle bark for tanning and vegetables for the markets in Tanga.

The Usambara hills are also the scene of much new European farming as the soil and

57  A Rendille family pause for water in the dry wastes of the
northern desert

climate has been found to be ideal for tea planting. Large new estates are being opened up on the high ridges and the quality of the tea produced is said to be as good as the best Ceylon.

To the east the Usambara Mountains run down to the coastal plain in a series of foothills. Here the moist sea winds condense in heavy rain and new estates are being planted with cocoa, a crop that was originally tried by the Germans and then abandoned until the Dutch, driven from the West Indies, revived it at Lugongo.

Throughout East Africa there are small tribes that do not fit into the general pattern around them; some are the old aboriginal inhabitants of the area, others are bands of migrants split off from the main stream of tribal movement. In addition to these there are the tribes of the Northern Frontier deserts of Kenya, true Hamites who came into the area from the 'Horn of Africa' and who have adapted themselves to the harsh conditions of this land.

The Northern Frontier District covers just over half the land area of Kenya but contains only three and a half per cent of the total population of the country at a density of under two persons per square mile. It is a land of blazing heat that beats back from the rocks and the bare ground in shimmering waves; where mountains thrust jagged splinters through the earth's crust as though the first phase of creation had only just ended. In this apparently hostile environment live the Boran and Rendille to the west, the Somali to the east. The whole of their life centres round their herds of cattle, camels, goats and fat-tailed Persian

58   The Uaso Nyiro river, showing the typical palm and thorn
scrub country of the north-east of Kenya

sheep. Their days are a constant rhythm of taking the stock to water (often at deep wells
where every bucketful has to be passed up a human chain from depths of 35 to 40 feet), then
moving them to grazing, then returning them to water. Surprisingly enough the animals are
of excellent quality, for the climate is almost sterile, with a complete absence of diseases,
and the water, whether from wells, springs or Lake Rudolf, has a high mineral content.

The Rendille moved into Kenya from the Ogaden, gradually travelling westwards until
they came against the barrier of Lake Rudolf, its waters constantly fretted by the hot winds,
set in a sinister landscape of black lava mountains and volcanoes. Here the Rendille settled,
finding water and grazing for their sheep and camels and co-existing fairly peacefully with
the Samburu to the south. It is an ascetic life, with a basic diet of camel's milk, some meat,
and blood drawn from the sheep and goats by cutting a vein in the neck, drawing off the
necessary amount and then plastering the wound with mud. They have few possessions
beyond their waterskins and the hides and skins that make their huts.

The Boran are a tribe allied to the Galla, the fierce Muslims who dominated the deserts
of Somalia and Abyssinia. They are cattle raisers who have developed their skill to such a
pitch that their cattle, raised in country that has no surface water and a minimum of grazing,
are prized both for their hardiness and their ability to produce first-class calves when bred
in the kinder areas to the south. The Boran still cling to their Muslim faith, and their habits

and lives are governed by it. They wear the long white cloaks that are common to tribes farther north and their women wear the black overall garments that are the badge of Muslim womanhood.

Related to the Boran are the Orma who live on either side of the Tana River. They have developed a white-skinned breed of cattle that has a great deterrent value against the tsetse fly that infests the area. The tsetse loves shade and darkness, and when it wants to rest or settle it always does so on dark objects. By breeding their cattle for white skins the Orma discouraged the settling of the fly on their hides, and so are able to pasture their herds in the fly-infested scrub land that borders the banks of the river. The Orma live in the same area as the Pokomo, a Bantu tribe of agriculturalists, and the relationship between these two tribes is of major importance for usually in Africa every tribe is jealous of its land and will allow no incursion, but over the centuries the Orma and Pokomo have developed side by side, each exploiting a different part of their common land.

The Tana River rises on the eastern slopes of the Aberdare Mountains and runs through the densely populated Kikuyu Highlands. It makes a loop southwards from Karatina past Fort Hall to swing then in a complete half circle northwards before turning once again south to the Indian Ocean at Kipini. The river is thus fed with the rain from both the Aberdares and Mount Kenya and collects annually the thousands of tons of rich topsoil washed off these highlands. This soil is deposited along its banks in the lower reaches where the river meanders over the plains and the flow of water is slow enough to let the silt settle out. During the floods, which occur after the two periods of rain up country, the river spills out over its flood plain and here the Pokomo plant their crops of rice and cassava. In places, where the river has made wide 'ox-bow' meanders the Pokomo have cut new channels across the base of the meander and use the old river bed as farm land that yields heavy crops from the fertile silt which is left. The fertility is replenished by allowing the flood waters into the ox-bow to irrigate it and deposit new soil. When the flood waters recede there are many pools of water left behind and in these the Pokomo find a plentiful supply of fish to augment their diet, while in the River Tana itself there are hippopotamus and crocodile, both of which are relished by them.

On the southern shores of Lake Rudolf live one of the smallest tribes in the world, the El Molo. They are a survival of the old original inhabitants of East Africa, the descendants of *Homo habilis*, and like the other remaining aboriginal races they owe their survival to the inhospitability of their surroundings, existing in conditions that would prove unacceptable to any other tribe. It is believed that there are only about ninety men, women and children left. They live in primitive shelters of grass and leaves right on the shores of the lake. There is no shelter or shade from the sun which beats down relentlessly on the lava rocks that cover the ground. The heat so generated causes a constant wind to blow from the cooler waters of the lake. Their diet is a monotonous one of fish which are plentiful in the lake despite its alkalinity. All attempts to move these remnants to a more hospitable environment have failed, and they cling staunchly to their own way of life, wanting no change.

The most widespread of the aboriginal tribes is the Wandorobo, for they occur in both Kenya and Tanganyika. They are not numerous but are found in the rain forests of the Aberdares and Mount Kenya, living in the forests of the Mau and scattered over most of the Masai areas of Tanganyika. It is with the Masai that the Dorobo have established the closest relationship, though they are also welcomed in the Kikuyu and Nandi lands. The Masai acknowledge the oldness of the Dorobo by their legend of the creation of man. According to them the first man in the world was a Dorobo and after he had looked it over and seen the animals and cattle he lay down and made a boy and a girl from each of his shin bones, and these were the first Masai.

The Dorobo live in the deep forests or the open bushlands, shunning contacts with the outside world, living with the animals so that they have an ability to track and understand them that appears magical to the European, and even other African tribes. Their needs are few and mostly satisfied from the forests in which they live – skins for covering and as blankets against the cold, bow and arrows, a gourd for snuff, primitive knives of iron, these are all the necessities of their life. They can manufacture poison for their arrows from the trees in the forest and make new strings of hide or wild sansevieria for their bows. So armed they can exist for ever, or as long as there are game animals, roots and berries. For not only are they unrivalled trackers and hunters, they are also possessed of a complete knowledge of all the plants that can be used by man. In the forest areas water is no problem, but for many years the ability of the Dorobo to live for long periods in waterless bush was a mystery. In fact it has been found that they exist on the roots of a certain plant that has only three or four very small leaves above the surface of the ground. The Dorobo dig up the roots of this plant which are like a potato but as big as a large water melon. They then either pound the flesh in a gourd, when it exudes a large amount of watery liquid, or simply chew large chunks of it to extract the juice. Perhaps the most amazing thing about the Dorobo is the symbiotic relationship that they have built up with *Indicator indicator*, a small brown bird of rather undistinguished appearance whose function is described in its common name of Honey Guide. This bird is addicted to honey, but as most bees in the wild build their combs in hollow trees or old ants' nests into which the bird cannot penetrate, it needs an agent to get the honey out. Having located a wild hive, the bird searches for the nearest human; it then flies round and round, calling and making short flights into the bush; as soon as the human starts to follow, the bird will lead the way, alternately flying and hopping from bough to bough until the hive is reached. The Dorobo will then excavate the honey and after taking his share will leave an adequate supply on the ground for the bird to feast upon. There is a very general belief amongst all Africans that if you are greedy and take all the honey, without leaving any for the Honey Guide, he will come back again one day and lead you straight to a poisonous snake. Unlike so many of the myths and stories of African wild life the story of the Honey Guide is completely true; the actions have been noted by many ornithologists of repute and have even recently been filmed.

In Tanganyika there are two aboriginal tribes who have very strong resemblances to the true Bushmen of the Kalahari; they are the Kindiga and Wasandawe. They are both 'click speaking' tribes, that is, their speech abounds in strange gutturals and clicks just like the Bushmen. The Kindiga live in the dense bushland to the south-east of Lake Eyasi. The lake which is full of hippopotamus itself lies in a branch of the Great Rift Valley containing large herds of buffalo and elephant. The Kindiga have developed as phenomenal archers, carrying a bow over $6\frac{1}{2}$ feet long which it is impossible for an ordinary man to draw. The effort needed to draw this immense weapon has led to the Kindiga developing huge shoulder muscles. The Sandawe live to the south of the Kindiga in the hills of the Kondoa district. They are a tall, light-skinned people with fine features; originally hunters they have now taken up a mixed agriculture of stock raising and farming. The foundation of their herds was laid when they traded their women to their neighbours for cattle and goats, for the Sandawe women were famous for their looks and their fertility and so they commanded a handsome price amongst the pastoral tribes. The links between the Sandawe and the Bushmen are particularly strong for not only is the language similar, but in their area there are rock paintings that are remarkably like those found in Southern Africa.

Another small tribe that speak a strange tongue are the Mbulu, who live to the north of the Sandawe in the hills that lie between the main Rift Valley and Lake Eyasi. Their name means 'Babbler' in Swahili and their language proved almost incomprehensible to the early travellers in their area. They also are a tall and light-skinned people of Hamitic stock and they settled in the hills only two hundred years ago, having been travelling southwards and westwards from Lake Victoria before this.

The Mbulu live to the south of the area known to the Germans as the 'Winter Highlands', an area of great scenic beauty with several large mountains of volcanic origin, and one active volcano called by the Masai '*Ol donyo Lengai*' (The Mountain of God). The subterranean forces that have produced the volcanoes have also produced one of the world's most splendid sights, the great caldera of Ngorongoro. It is often mistakenly called a crater, but this is incorrect as a crater is the remains of the vent of a volcano, whilst a caldera is produced by the sinking of the earth's surface into the 'hole' produced by the movement away of molten rock. Whatever the technical name, it is one of the natural wonders of the world. One stands on the rim of a huge bowl, the far side almost lost in the distant blue haze. At one's feet the ground falls away for over a thousand feet to what looks like a green lawn until one's eye becomes accustomed to the scale and one realises that this is a plain,

59　A Mbulu homestead

dotted with lakes and trees and woods, that the specks are vast herds of wildebeeste and zebra. Driving round the edge one passes through rain forest with long streams of moss hanging from the trees and herds of elephant and buffalo in the thickets, then one plunges down a steep road to the floor of the cauldron and one is in a huge park, walled round with an escarpment hundreds of feet high, above which the sky is a dome that seems to rest on the rim of the hills. Great herds graze across the grassy plain with gazelles skipping and butting between them. Rhinos doze bad-temperedly in an area left respectfully clear by the other animals. On an anthill a pride of lions, their bellies uncomfortably distended with food, lie on their backs suffering the agonies of gluttony, while everywhere there are birds. Lovely crested cranes, their wings flashing crimson as they dance their fantastic courtship display, their grey bodies and gold crests quivering in ecstasy; busy blacksmith plovers dashing about in their black and white livery with their metallic 'ting, ting, ting' that sounds just like the ring of dwarf hammers on an anvil; Egyptian geese in buff and red, sacred ibis in black-edged white and the lovely pure white cattle egret collect by the pools; whilst overhead flash the bee-eaters and the starlings in an incandescence of purples and greens and carmines.

60   The rim of the Ngorongoro caldera with moss-covered rain forest on the top and dry grass savannah at the bottom

# 8 European Settlers and Urban Dwellers

THE PATTERNS OF EUROPEAN SETTLEMENT in the three countries of East Africa have been very different. This is due not only to the differing political conditions in the three territories but also differences in the climate and crops that could be grown.

By the Imperial Decree of November 1895, all the land in German East Africa was declared Crown Land, but the existing rights of individuals and of tribes were guaranteed. Because of the lack of communications the first areas to be developed were those on the Coast, so crops that could be planted in these conditions were eagerly sought. A few sisal plants had been imported from Florida in 1892. These did even better in their new location and soon sisal was the major plantation crop in German East Africa.

Sisal is a plant of the succulent *agave* family, with large fleshy leaves tipped with a strong thorn. After a period of growth when the leaves can attain a length of nearly six feet, the plant puts out a flower spike or 'pole' that grows to a height of ten or twelve feet. On this appear hundreds of small 'bulbils', bulbs with growing leaves, which are planted and mature as the next crop. The leaves are cut from the growing plant over a period of years starting with the lowest ring, then processed in a machine that scrapes away all the fleshy part of the leaf, leaving the fibre behind. This fibre is then dried and bleached in the sun and sold to spinners who produce rope and twine from it. Fluctuations in the world markets have made it a crop that at times has paid huge dividends, while at other times it has barely been worth producing, but for many years it was the staple crop of the Tanganyika economy.

Sisal is a true plantation crop as it needs a fairly large labour force but not much supervision. The German estates spread inland from Tanga, round the base of the Usambara Mountains. Then in 1907 when the Central Railway line was started from Dar-es-Salaam, new areas suitable for sisal were discovered round the base of the Uluguru Mountains at Morogoro and on the Mkondowa River at Kilosa. Very soon the demand for labour could no longer be supplied from the tribes living round the sisal plantations and indentured labourers had to be imported from Portuguese East Africa and Southern Tanganyika to do the work required.

At the same time that the sisal industry was starting up, the German Government made large alienations of land in the Usambara Mountains and on the foothills of Kilimanjaro. In the Usambaras a forestry and tropical research station was established at Amani and a settlement built in the hills at Wilhelmstal (now called Lushoto). Coffee, rubber and cinchona trees (for quinine) were all grown with some success, but the soil was not really suitable for coffee and it was only with the introduction of tea (after the last war) that the area was really developed to its full capacity, though there had always been a very flourishing timber industry with both teak and mahogany being cut and milled.

On the foothills of Kilimanjaro the conditions were ideal for coffee, and the plantations

61 Sisal growing in a plantation near Kilosa

62 Cutting the leaf

prospered so that the German Government took over the privately built railway from Tanga to the Usambaras and pushed it through to Moshi in 1912 in order to facilitate the export of the crop.

Round Morogoro and Kilosa, in addition to sisal, the Germans planted cotton. The inability of the American growers to supply European demand at the turn of the century encouraged this industry and also led to the Germans making seed and instructions on cultivation available to the Africans in the plains of the Rufiji River.

The aim of the German policy was primarily to produce materials for their home industries and they encouraged settlement by any nationality willing to work the land. In addition to Germans there were Greek, Italian, Danish, Dutch, Swedish and French settlers in the early days. Indeed the Germans even alienated land for the plantation growing of rubber to English companies, despite the vigorous protests of their own nationals. The cosmopolitan atmosphere engendered by this settlement policy stood the country in very good stead and prevented the formation of the 'white supremacist' clique that was to become such a trouble in Kenya. Future relations between the settlers and the Africans were helped by the fact that the Germans, in the Imperial Decree of 1895, committed themselves to leaving four times as much land as was in current occupation by any tribe free for future expansion of that tribe.

We have seen in Chapter 3 that the primary reason for opening up British East Africa to settlement was the need to make the expensive investment of the Uganda Railway pay. After the granting of the huge tract of Masai land to Lord Delamere, very few other applications for land were made, so the Kenya Government sent their Commissioner of Customs to South Africa to attempt to attract settlers. The response was immediate and for the next six years there was a steady stream of settlers trekking up from South Africa, their trek carts piled high with household goods, seeds, ploughs and all the necessities for starting

63   Stripping the fibre
from the leaf

64   Collecting the dried
sisal fibre

a farm; spans of oxen straining to pull the laden wagons over the plains, up the escarpments to the highlands on the edge of the Rift Valley. The Boer settlers were matched by a trickle of British, but there were many hold-ups in allocating land and incessant disputes as to the terms on which land could be taken up.

Despite this uncertainty, land was soon made productive and wheat, potatoes and coffee were grown in quantities sufficient for some export before the First World War intervened. The first coffee had been introduced into Kenya by John Patterson of the Scottish Mission at Kibwezi in 1893, but most of the seedlings died and the real start of the Kenya coffee industry was a plantation of 100 seedlings made by Brother Solanus Zipper of the St Austin's Mission of Nairobi. Most of the early settler plantations were started with seed from the St Austin's site, and in 1909 eight and a half tons of coffee (value £236) were exported from Kenya.

After the war the old settlers came back to derelict and overgrown farms, whilst new settlers poured into the country, many sponsored by the Discharged Soldiers Settlement Scheme that enabled ex-servicemen to obtain land with assisted bank loans. Prospects were extremely rosy, with the price of all primary products high, and flax, which was the quick-return crop that most new settlers were planting, standing at £500 per ton. The slump of 1921 was an appalling blow to the economy. Flax dropped to £100 per ton, all other prices followed suit and the final disaster was the drought of 1922 that destroyed the coffee crop. Many settlers went bankrupt, those who remained were crippled for years by debts, mortgages and loans at extortionate interest rates.

Just as the farms were beginning to get on a sound footing again, the world-wide slump of 1929 hit them. Prices again tumbled, development of new crops and the opening up of new areas had to stop. The farmers reverted to a subsistence economy growing their own food, bartering the surplus, watching mortgage interest pile up in arrears at the banks, who dared not foreclose on what was at that time a worthless investment. Gradually the economic pendulum swung back, money eased as tourists began to come to the country to shoot the game that abounded everywhere.

The Second World War gave a great push to the economy. Instead of the stagnation of the previous war, there was expansion as Kenya became the main base for the Ethiopian Campaign and Kilindini home port for the Indian Ocean Fleet. The impetus was kept up after the war and the settlers entered into the full flowering of their efforts. It was a just reward for the years of faith and hard, unremitting toil that had gone before.

Much has been written in derogation of the white settlers in Kenya, but it is well to remember the sheer driving endeavour that they put into their dream of turning a bit of Africa into a reasonable facsimile of England. In one lifetime they brought a change in the landscape unparalleled since the early enclosures in England. They took the African environment, worked on it with love and devotion and made it a European home. There is nothing African in the grassy hills, woods and undulating fields of Molo and Mau Summit, or the rolling wheatfields of the Escarpment, or the lush green grass and herbaceous borders of the Kinangop and Karen. It was perhaps the unconscious expression of a deep desire to keep Africa out, to create a walled garden into which to slip away from the reality of the world outside.

Whatever the reason, the end-product of the hard work was extremely pleasant. In the morning the farmer would be out at dawn, the air raw, smoke from the African huts lying in a blue haze round the wet thatch, wisps of mist curling up from the river. He would get the work of the farm started, perhaps ride round the gangs at work, then back to breakfast and any office work necessary. In the middle of the morning, the sun would be warm enough to walk about without a sweater, the heat would bring out the smell of red dust and the rising tang of cypress. There would be the thump of a tractor working, the lowing of cattle and the sharp cry of a circling buzzard. By mid-afternoon most of the work would be finished

65   Safari. Tent, camp chair, table and water filter; home for much of the year for the government officials who guided and administered the territories

96

66   The harvest starts on a 'Highland' farm in Kenya

and the farm silent and sleepy with heat, the distant views veiled in a deep, shivering delphinium-blue haze. Then as the sun went down across the Rift the farm would come to life again. Cooking fires would be lighted and there would be a chatter of talk. The air would chill with a hint of frost and the farmer would sprawl before a roaring log fire in a great stone fireplace, the room littered with dogs, cats, vases of flowers and old and well-loved furniture.

It was a way of life that would perhaps have changed of its own accord as the old generation who had created it died. But the change has been hastened by the emergency, the attainment of Independence, and the new agricultural policy. As a result of the Lancaster House Conference of 1960 the 'White Highlands' policy in Kenya was abandoned and it was decided to use one-third of the good European farming land to settle African farmers. This 'Million acre project' transformed many of the old farm areas. Large fields, paddocks, pasture land and farm buildings have been carved into small seven- to twenty-acre farms, each with its corrugated-iron-roofed huts. A landscape that for a brief period was maturely European is being changed once more to African.

Many of the European settlers whose farms have been bought have stayed, with their sons, to become settlement officers, carving up their own land and helping the Africans to take over. Many have returned to England or the older parts of the Commonwealth, and there are some who are still farming in Kenya, for there are still $2\frac{1}{2}$ million acres of farmland

97

producing every kind of agricultural product from some of the fattest and best managed farmland in the world.

Town life as a concept was completely foreign to the African until well into this century. There were the coastal towns and a few trading centres inland such as Tabora and Ujiji; there were the 'royal' towns of the Kingdoms of Uganda such as Kampala, Kabarole and Hoima; but apart from these, the African lived scattered over the land in small family groups. The coming of systematic administration created the towns of East Africa, siting them along the lines of communication.

It is interesting to see the differences in town design thrown up by the differences in outlook of the two powers who controlled East Africa. The German town grew up round its *Boma* or Fort. This occupied a commanding position, with the streets radiating from it so they could be swept with gunfire from the walls of the fort. The *Boma* itself was built round a square with thick walls that rose to battlements and crenellations; often there was a tower and flagstaff over the gate which was closed with a heavy teak door plentifully sprinkled with brass and iron studs. Within the walls were the offices of the District Commissioner, Police, the *Akida*, the native treasury and living quarters for some of the Europeans. The *Boma* was the first thing built in a new settlement and round its whitewashed walls there grew up a town that started as mud huts and gradually developed as trade and wealth increased. *Bomas* were often sited with an amazing flair for effect. Tabora growing out of a hilltop like a Crusader castle; Dodoma planted at the crossing of the railway and north–south trunk route with a coldly calculated field of fire from its walls; Pangani standing in a grove of palms and casuarinas; grass lawns, bougainvillaeas and frangipani stretching to the river's edge with a view past the wharf and Customs House out to the breakers and the blue Indian Ocean. Most of the posts grew, but there are some that died. All that remain standing are the gaunt walls with trees growing from the mud bricks and bats roosting in the caverns that were once rooms. There are many tales of these deserted *Bomas* – of lights that move over the battlements, of cries and shouts, the stamp of boots and chink of swords at night. They are shunned as the abode of restless spirits. Even in the sunlight there is an oppressiveness within their walls.

In the British Territories the first building in a town was usually a shop or hotel and the administration was carried out from a small timber and corrugated-iron hut. Whilst the town developed and shops, hotels and clubs were built in stone and brick with tiled roofs, government was still carried on from ancient timber buildings. For some years the Legislative Council of Kenya met in the Railway Institute and Club in Nairobi, a corrugated-iron shanty, and as late as 1950 many of the principal Government departments were housed in single-storey wooden sheds, raised on piles above the ground.

The result of this difference of approach is very apparent in the form of the town today. The ex-German towns have a compact and visually coherent centre with a sense of purpose; an order about the placing of shops, hotels and offices that makes the town have a logic as a place. The British towns are a straggle of buildings (quite often down one long street) with no coherence and even less basic plan. One has only to compare the order of Dar-es-Salaam, with the Government buildings, flanked by churches, hotels and the shopping area; to the chaos of Nairobi, with Government offices scattered all over the town; or at a lower level the long wiggles of Nakuru and Eldoret with the clean planning of Dodoma and Arusha.

The transition to an urban life has been very hard for the African, for not only has he had to make the adjustment within a generation, he has also had to accommodate a great change in the form of the town during this period. Until comparatively recently most of the larger towns had an area of African housing that could be called nothing but a shanty town. There was little Municipal house building and what there was went to Government or Municipal employees. The rest had to find accommodation as best they could, with little or no capital or income for building a home. The new arrival from the country, drawn to the town by tales of work and money, would start out as a lodger in a boarding house or 'hoteli' in which he shared a room with four or five others for about two or three shillings a week (on a weekly income of twelve to twenty shillings). This sum provided the roof over his head and the walls. He had to find all his own bedding (often his own bed) and all his own food. If he got on well he would bring his wife from his home village and they would rent a room of their own, eventually getting a small plot of land and building on it a mud and wattle house with corrugated-iron or thatch roof; a hut was a couple of extra rooms which they in turn could let off to lodgers to make more money. The African housing areas seldom had any drainage, water was often only available from a stand-pipe at street corners, electric light was practically unknown. The progression to better housing conditions was solely dependent upon a person's wealth and for every one who climbed up the economic ladder there were hundreds who made no progress at all. These unfortunates lived in bothies of sacking, beaten-out petrol tins and grass thatch that clustered round the outskirts of the town. Without sanitation, surrounded by dirt, in the grip of an economic thraldom that paid only subsistence wages; it is small wonder that these slums bred despair and disaffection.

One of the very worst effects of the rapid urbanisation of the African was his loss of tribal identity. In his own lands he was a person, a member of a family, a sub-clan, a clan,

67   An Indian housewife shops for vegetables in Dar-es-Salaam

a tribe. He had an exact orientation within the tribal structure and was known by everyone he met in his daily life. All this was taken from him as soon as he went to live in a town. He became an anonymous unit, working with men of many different tribes, with varying customs and beliefs. His work had little or no connection with the rest of his life.

In the towns the huge gulf between the African and the European and Indian became suddenly apparent to the newcomer. In his own land he had been used to a basic egalitarianism that respected tribal hierarchies but which was founded on a true community of interests and a complete mutual respect. In the town he had to grapple with a social order based on assumptions of superiority and inferiority, reinforced by an economy that would seem to be directly aimed at perpetuating the divisions between the races. It was not only in the obvious differences of housing, transport and opportunity that the sense of being someone apart lay but also in small signs, such as the fact that most Europeans gave their dogs four times as much meat per week as they gave their servants; that while they could drink unlimited alcohol the African had to have a permit to brew his own beer.

The detribalising effect of urban life was painful and although, with Independence, many of the barriers have been swept away, the fact still remains that living in a town is basically against the traditions of African life. As the towns expand and more and more people come to live in them there will have to be a serious effort to bridge the gap between the newcomer and the town liver. The recurrence of tribal factions in politics is perhaps an indication of the desire to retain some links with the homeland – exactly analogous to the formation of Societies of St George, St David and St Andrew in the expatriate British population.

The Asian community has dominated the commercial world in East Africa, providing nearly all the shopkeepers as well as the clerks, accountants and foremen necessary to run the country. In the early days they lived over their shops, a tradition that has continued, so that many new shops in the cities have flats as well as offices built over them. With increasing wealth the Asian moves out of the town centre and builds in a peripheral suburb. He has retained his preference for a distinctly oriental style of architecture, with flat roofs, curved walls, balconies, deep verandahs and ornamental windows. The grouping of nationalities into particular areas in towns has been encouraged not only by legislation such as the Kenya 'White Highlands' restriction of ownership in certain areas to Europeans only, but also by the rigid zoning of areas for high-density, medium-density and low-density housing.

Just as distinctive as the areas of 'Bombay Baroque' architecture with the clash of green, pink and yellow colour-washed walls and curling ironwork decoration, are the areas of 'Expatriate Elizabethan' created by the British colony. The grey stone walls, mullioned and leaded windows, timber and brick porches, red tiled roofs and large fireplaces were signs of the desire to shut out the surroundings and create a false environment in a country that was felt unconsciously to be hostile.

The distrusts and misunderstandings between the races of Africa were magnified by the rigid hierarchical divisions in the large towns, where African, Asian and European met only at work. As soon as the evening came they went to their own areas, mixed only with their own kind. The African to talk politics in beer hall and smoky mud hut; the Asian to stroll with friends in the cool of the evening, the saris of the women making bright splashes of colour in the dusty air; the European to golf, the Club, and the flicker of a log fire in the hearth. The larger the town, the more rigid were the divisions, the more inflexible the segregation beween the races.

The granting of Independence has not swept away the sociological problem of three totally different ethnic groups trying to live together. If it was wrong to live separately, making no attempt to reach a basic community pattern, then it is just as wrong to try to impose a common standard on all. It is only when this particular problem is solved and the urban dwellers recognise themselves as equal individual citizens of one city, that true partnership will have been achieved.

68   A shopping street in the old town of Zanzibar

# 9 Zanzibar and Dar-es-Salaam

AS ONE APPROACHES THE ISLAND OF ZANZIBAR, one suddenly smells a sharp, exciting, aromatic smell, a smell that someone once said reminded them of apple-pies and toothaches. It is the smell of cloves, bagged and ready for export crammed into the warehouses of the town, for Zanzibar is the centre of the clove trade, producing and exporting more cloves than any other country in the world. This trade has brought wealth and prosperity to the island, but since the earliest days, it has always been an important town, playing a major part in the story of East Africa. It has always been prosperous, first in its association with Kilwa and the Zimbabwe gold trade, then as the seat of the Sultan of Muscat, the centre of the slave trade and of a commercial network that reached inland to the lakes. A network so well maintained that the old saying has it that 'When they pipe in Zanzibar, they dance at Tabora.'

Zanzibar is the largest of the islands off the coast of East Africa, and its name is a corruption of the old Arabic for the whole of the Coast – the *Zinj-el-barr*, or land of the blacks. To the north is the island of Pemba, whose Arabic name *Al Khudhra*, 'the Green Island', exactly describes the lush vegetation that is found on both islands. Life must always have been easy, with the plentiful rainfall, the sweet fresh water, the sea teeming with hundreds of varieties of fish, the land growing coconuts, maize, bananas, manioc, rice and dates, also supporting large herds of goats and sheep. Standing in the ruins of one of the old palaces outside the town, with the bathing-pools filled with water-lilies, the sun filtering through the green canopy of palm leaves and glinting on the sea, one recaptures the essence of Scheherazade's tales of Sinbad and his wanderings; of a vanished, leisured and complex civilisation.

The town of Zanzibar echoes these feelings, for of all the towns in East Africa it is the least African. The high stone buildings stand along narrow twisting alleys, secretive behind massive carved doorways, shuttered windows and heavily latticed balconies. In the alleyways are small shops, their wares spilling out into the lane where Africans, Indians and Arabs jostle together, the only traffic a donkey or a rattling cart piled high with sacks and pushed by two or three running Africans shouting for room to pass. It might be a part of Bombay, Baghdad or Basra. The glory of this part of the stone town is the number of old carved doors, which have always been the outward sign of the wealth of the owner of the house. The doors themselves are carved with geometric patterns and heavily studded with huge nails, either of iron or brass, which are kept highly polished. The purpose of the nails is now purely decorative but they are a remembrance of similar doors in India and the Middle East which were studded in this fashion so that attacking elephants could not batter the doors down with their heads. The door-frames are intricately carved with fishes and waves and entwined with flowers. The whole is kept oiled so that the wood goes almost

black. It is quite usual for one door to be so thick that it weighs several hundredweight, but so skilfully balanced on a pivot that it can be opened and shut by a small child.

The old town was originally built (like Mombasa and the other Arabic cities) on an island for defensive reasons, but the lagoon that once separated it from the mainland has been filled in to provide a park and playing fields. On the seaward side of the island there is a broad open space called the Maidan, with fountains, *Acacia* trees and some old cannons pointing out to sea. Flanking the Maidan are the walls of the old Omani/Arabic fort; the palace of the Sultan of Zanzibar, a white building with crenellations rather like a children's fort; and in the centre, the *Beit-al-Ajaib*, or House of Wonders. This was built by the Sultan Seyyid Bargash in 1883 as a palace, on the site of the house of his father the first Sultan. It has a number of carved doors that are acknowledged to be the finest ever made and a staircase with real silver knobs on the banisters. It was called the House of Wonders not because of any of these, however, but because it had the first, and until quite recently, the only, lift in Zanzibar. This was an ancient and marvellous contraption of open ironwork that clanked, whirred and groaned up and down, emitting sparks and flashes from its primitive electric motor. It was, in its way, as impressive a symbol as the large scarlet Rolls Royce, in which the Sultan was ceremoniously driven about the island.

The clove tree was introduced to Zanzibar by Seyyid Said. He obtained some seedlings of clove trees from a French collector in Mauritius called Poivre who had imported them to grow in the botanical gardens he was setting up. The seedlings did extremely well, as the moist warm climate of Zanzibar suited them. When he saw this the Sultan ordered all the Arab landholders in the island to plant clove trees, making it compulsory for them to plant three seedlings for each coconut tree they owned. Although the order was very unpopular, no one dared not comply with it, as the Sultan was all-powerful and had said that he would confiscate the estate of anybody who disobeyed him. This autocratic action proved to be a

70   The 'House of Wonders' overlooking the Maidan at Zanzibar.
Note that the clock on the tower shows Swahili time which is
recorded from sunrise to sunset, i.e. the time shown as 7.25 is
actually 1.25 pm

blessing, for the trees throve and within thirty years Zanzibar had a monopoly of the clove
trade.

The clove grows on a fairly large tree with an attractive shape and dark shining leaves
rather like a bay. The clove is the unopened bud of the flower and it is picked when green,
spread out in the sun to dry and, when it is quite black, packed for export. Some flowers are
always left on each tree, and they come out deep-cream coloured and star-shaped, with a
heavy smell. Unlike the coconut plantations which are usually laid out in regular lines, the
clove plantations have trees planted in no kind of order except when they line a road or
track. In Pemba, which has the finest plantations, the groves are like an English wood, with
the silvery boles of the trees dappled with flecks of sunlight filtering through the dense
foliage. Harvesting is a primitive business, everyone turns out and hordes of casual labour
flock on to the Islands from the mainland, often making the crossing in tiny outrigger
canoes, for the pay is good while the harvest lasts.

During the Portuguese occupation of the Coast Pemba was an important settlement,
providing food for both Mombasa and Mozambique. The Portuguese settlers on the island
became infamous for their treachery and deceitfulness. They had a local law that decreed
that any chicken straying into the compound of a Portuguese became his property, as it was
obviously a Christian convert! But after the defeat of the Portuguese, the island slipped back
into an unobtrusive existence, though the inhabitants still practise a form of bull-fighting
that is a relic of the old days.

Zanzibar is unlike any other part of East Africa, for it is the only place where the past is constantly about one – not the recent past, but a millennium of occupation that has left its traces in the buildings and in the people. There are the Hadima, the fishing tribe of the East Coast who are the relic of the old Bantu inhabitants, with a large bone structure and a curious language of their own. There are the descendants of the slaves, so that Zanzibari Africans can be seen with the typical features of many of the tribes of the interior of Africa. There are the Indian families that trace their line back to the original traders of the seventeenth century, and the Arabs who still retain their distinctive dress and finely chiselled features. Perhaps the two most moving relics in the Island are the old slave-pit on the beach at Mangapwani, where the slaves were penned like cattle, awaiting shipment that would mean death during the voyage to at least half of them, and the Cathedral at Zanzibar.

It is built on the site of the old slave market and it stands in a kind of close, withdrawn from the bustle and turmoil of the old town. There are deep shade trees around it and the green darkness is a welcome change from the glare of the lime-washed walls in the alleys outside. The Cathedral was built by Bishop Steere, who designed it, trained all the craftsmen who built it, and who lies buried behind the High Altar that he placed exactly on the site where the whipping post of the slave market had been. Here in the dim interior one feels all the threads of the past suddenly come together: there is a sense of a continuity that stretches from the turbulent old to the prosperous new.

Sultan Majid bin Said founded Dar-es-Salaam in 1866 as a refuge from possible trouble in Zanzibar. Despite the loyalty shown to him when he first ascended the throne his position was basically very insecure and he was always frightened of a revolt amongst his subjects or overthrow by Oman. He therefore chose a completely fresh site for his refuge on the mainland about twenty miles south of Bagamoyo on a perfect natural harbour. He named this new town Dar-es-Salaam, which means 'Haven of Peace', and wished it to become the main port for trade with the Lakes. When he died in 1870 and was succeeded by Seyyid Bargash the development of the town was stopped, for Bargash was not interested in a possible second capital.

The advantages of the harbour and the line of communication with the trading towns inland brought Arabs and Indians to settle in the town and in 1877 Bargash gave Sir William Mackinnon (who was the founder of the British India Line) and Sir Thomas Buxton permission to build a road from Dar-es-Salaam to Lake Nyasa to open up trade with that region without having to go through Portuguese territory. Work on this road proceeded very slowly and it was finally abandoned in 1881 after seventy miles had been built, as it was found that the tsetse fly made it impossible to use any form of animal-drawn transport. The promise of the road had, however, encouraged many more traders to settle in the port, so that by 1880 it had a thriving commercial community, an Arab Governor appointed by the Sultan and a Customs House for the payment of dues.

With the coming of the Germans Dar-es-Salaam began to grow apace. Apart from the German administrators there was an influx of missionaries. The Lutherans arrived first and built their mission out on the point near the harbour entrance; they were soon followed by the Benedictine Fathers who settled on land at Kurasini Creek, an inland arm of the harbour. Along the curve of the bay the Germans placed their Government offices, *Boma* and church. Behind this front were built shops and hotels to serve the new community and houses for the Europeans. These old German houses were adapted from the Arab houses of Zanzibar. They were built five or six feet above the ground, raised on a series of vaulted arches; steps led on to a deep verandah that ran all round the house with rooms opening off it through arches. The walls, of coral rag and lime plaster, were three to four feet thick and windows were left to a minimum so that the interior of the house was always dark and cool. During the hot weather grass matting was let down over the front of the verandah and left soaked with water, which further cooled the house by its evaporation. The Germans planted the streets with rows of flamboyant *Acacia* trees and started a botanical garden and park.

Dar-es-Salaam has been called, rightly, one of the most perfect harbours in the world. The best way to approach the town is from the sea, for then the full drama of its situation bursts on one. The ship approaches the shore head-on, to the right a long coastline of dazzling beaches backed by palms and casuarina trees, the white birthday-cake crenellations of the old Government House (now called State House) dominating the scene; to the left a tangle of dark mangroves and a lighthouse. The ship appears to be driving straight on to the shore, less than a hundred yards away are bathers and fishermen on the beaches; she enters a narrow channel with the land close on either hand, then suddenly, with a turn to starboard, she is through into the circular bay, completely landlocked, with no view of the sea. As the final berthing manœuvres are made there is time to take in the details of this most lovely lagoon. A great sweep of sand in the foreground, then the green of palm trees and flamboyants with their scarlet flowers break up the pattern of the buildings that curl round the waterfront. Massive old German Government buildings contrast with modern offices and hotels, their walls flashing with colours and patterned with deep shadows in the strong vertical sunlight. The curving panorama is punctuated by the towers of the Lutheran Church and the spire of the Catholic Cathedral; it sweeps round to the shining silver maze of pipes and oil tanks inseparable from any waterfront, then to the deep-water berths built on the site of the old dhow harbour.

Behind this façade lies a thriving and bustling capital city which has expanded greatly in population and size since the end of the last war. The first wave of expansion was the influx of colonial officials and businessmen that poured into the country in the late forties and early fifties. A new tract of housing land was created from an old sisal plantation and the suburb of Oyster Bay grew from the solid coral. Standard pattern Government houses set in individual gardens of up to a quarter of an acre were interspersed with plots let for private development. In the years that have elapsed the rawness of much of this quick development has been hidden by tree planting and the fantastic power of the bougainvillaea to thrive on almost solid rock and provide a luxuriant cover of deep green leaves and purple flowers.

The odd British passion for gardening in even the most inhospitable of environments has triumphed once again. Waste water from bath and sink is carefully channelled across beds of almost pure coral sand to irrigate paw-paw trees and ornamental bushes of variegated croton, frangipani, oleander and hibiscus. Petunias, marigolds and zinnias add deep patches of ground colour, whilst aloes and *Euphorbia* thrive in the dry conditions and provide exotic flowers to rival the more homely blooms.

71 Dar-es-Salaam. This aerial view shows the narrow entrance to the harbour and the regular street pattern imposed by the Germans

The second wave was composed of the businessmen who came to help the developing economy during the fifties; some needed houses as they were staying to build up local branches but most were transients paying visits to their local agents; there was also a growing tourist industry. These new demands fostered the need for new hotels and there was a minor boom as it was fulfilled. Hotels were built in the heart of the town or along the coastal road to Oyster Bay. At the same time blocks of flats were springing up in the centre of the town to cater for the longer-staying transients so that the area behind the Azania Front developed upwards, ten-storey buildings replacing two-storey houses and shops.

The third wave was the result of Independence, composed of the large missions bearing gifts, blandishments, promises and aid that descend on any newly emergent nation, the experts that are sent by the United Nations to help the country develop and the volunteer corps that come to give their help in the work. But Dar-es-Salaam has also become the focus for the forces of Pan-Africanism. Here are nationalists from most of the countries of Southern Africa plotting and scheming for the day when they will free their peoples from white domination. The coffee shops and houses are full of a ferment of talk, idealism, and the cold practicalities of subversion and revolt. This last wave has strained the town to its limit and there is a serious shortage of accommodation, for although the capital investment needed to provide for the second wave was readily forthcoming in a time of prosperity and stability, the present uncertainty is inhibiting the investment necessary to meet this latest demand.

In an arc that runs from west to north behind the town centre is the African township, a great sprawl of housing that ranges from sturdily built bungalows to palm-thatch and kerosene-tin shacks. Here live the local tribe, the Wazaramo, a happy and traditionally gay people with a reputation for easy-going fecklessness and tolerance. To them have been added half the races of the country, drawn to the capital for work or political reasons.

The streets are busy and crowded, giving a cross-section of the community. Traditional Swahili walk through the pushing throng in long white robes and skull caps jostled by others more modern in slacks and shirts or sometimes a West African in flowing and colourful robes. The women are a kaleidoscope of coloured cotton prints, some worn as dresses, some as sarongs. Here and there is a Muslim woman still wearing the black *bui-bui* or head-to-toe veil that does in fact make them look like the spider which *bui-bui* means in Swahili. More often than not nowadays the veil is thrown back off the face and the *bui-bui* becomes little more than a cloak round the shoulders. Mixed into this crowd are Arab dhow captains with silver daggers at their waists and turbans on their heads, Indian traders sitting at their open shops, their wares spread round them on sacks and old boxes, silent sari-clad women slipping through the streets with their marketing bags, and, perhaps, a few ochre-daubed Wagogo in red blankets wandering open-eyed round the town, having driven cattle down to the meat-packing factory from the burning plains of Ugogo.

The ear is assaulted by a continuous babel of speech, shouted instructions and yells for room as water-carriers with two drums yoked across their shoulders pad out to the parts of the town where water is still a luxury. Coffee-sellers with pots of bitter black coffee attract custom as they walk by rhythmically chinking the small coffee cups together, ice-cream sellers honk three- or four-note phrases on small bicycle bulb horns to advertise their wares and the charcoal-seller cries his goods with a long drawn '*Mka-a-a-a*' that sounds like a soul in torment. High above all this is the tinny blare of tunes from the radios and hand-wound gramophones that are found in every coffee house and food shop. The nose picks out the smell of baking bread and chapatties, maize being toasted on the pavement over a charcoal brazier, dried shark, dried fish, sticky cakes and sweetmeats, garlic, coriander, cumin and the sharp prickle of ground chillies, dust and hot humanity.

This is the basic brew from which the strength of Tanzania comes, the binding together of many tribes and races by the process of living with one another so that tribalism is relegated to its true unimportance and the people work together for one party, one Government, one all-embracing state.

73 Fruit-sellers in the municipal market. Oranges were first brought to the country by early traders from China. The mats on which the fruits are laid and the baskets in the background are made from palm leaves

72 The harbour front at Dar-es-Salaam. The Catholic Cathedral stands in the centre of the picture, with the Lutheran church on the right

# 10 Kampala and Nairobi

OF ALL THE CITIES OF EAST AFRICA Kampala is the only one that has always been a capital of one sort or another, though the name Kampala dates from the meeting between Lugard and the Kabaka Mwanga. For many years before the coming of the Europeans the Kings of Buganda had lived on hills in the area, not only because they gave good defensive positions, but also because hilltops gave prestige at a time when all water had to be carried from the nearest river, so obviously the farther a man was from the river the more affluent he was, for he could afford many wives to carry the water that far. Each Kabaka chose a different hill for his *Lubiri* or royal enclosure, but as there were so many hills round what is now Kampala, and re-building it was a huge undertaking, the *Lubiri* never moved far. Since Mwanga's time the *Lubiri* has not moved from Mengo Hill.

When Lugard arrived the top of Mengo Hill was crowned with a palisade of elephant grass, the bundles crossed in a diagonal pattern which only the Kabaka was allowed to use. Inside this palisade was a town of over a thousand grass huts ranging in size from the royal apartments down to the small huts of aged and pensioned retainers. At the gate burnt the sacred *Gombolola* fire, only extinguished at the death of the Kabaka. Within this palisade was also the parliament hall of the Baganda and other halls of audience. Lugard was not the first European to visit the *Lubiri*, for he had been preceded by Speke, Grant and Stanley, and at the time of his arrival there were both Protestant and Roman Catholic missionaries in residence around Mengo. Lugard who had been sent to negotiate a treaty with the Kabaka had had a difficult march from the Coast, and he records in his diary that he was hard put to it to muster decent clothes to wear to impress the Kabaka. He finally settled upon a pair of cord breeches and pyjama jacket that had brass buttons on it. In this ceremonial outfit, accompanied by some of the troops he had brought with him and a bugler to sound the fanfare, he called officially on the Kabaka. Whether it was the impressiveness of Lugard's clothes or some other factor the treaty was eventually signed and on 13 January 1891 the Kabaka gave to Lugard a small hill called Kampala on which to make his headquarters. It is perhaps significant that of all the hills round Mengo, Kampala is the lowest, and the Kabaka's generosity may quite possibly also have contained a subtle insult that would have been well appreciated by his subjects. The name Kampala means 'the place of the Impala' and Lugard at once christened it Fort Kampala and proceeded to build a stockaded post there.

From these beginnings modern Kampala has grown, a city that sprawls over the many hills in the area, and so one that has an individuality and element of surprise that is lacking in the formal grid-iron layouts of Dar-es-Salaam and Nairobi. On top of each hill stands an important building, so that when one looks across at the city there is a monumental air about it with each hill crowned with an imposing building on which to focus the eye.

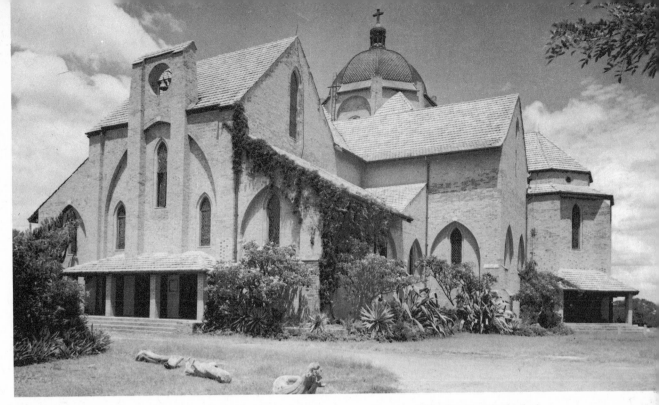

74 Namirembe Cathedral

On Namirembe Hill stands the Protestant Cathedral of St Paul, built by the Church Missionary Society. The first missionary arrived in Buganda in 1877, a young Scottish engineer called Mackay who had been working in Germany when he was chosen to lead the party to Africa at the early age of twenty-six. It was only a few weeks after he arrived and had made the first overtures to the Kabaka Mutesa that a rival party of missionaries consisting of Roman Catholic White Fathers arrived at Mengo led by Father Simeon Lourdel who was twenty-three. The dismay of the Church Missionary Society party at this arrival can be imagined, for not only was it a 'Low Church' organisation, but Mackay was particularly anti-Catholic. At the first meeting between the Kabaka Mutesa and the two rival missions a terrible row occurred, for Lourdel was just as convinced in his opinions as Mackay. Both behaved very discreditably and Mutesa was driven to suggest to them that it would be better if they agreed amongst themselves as to who had the right religion before trying to convert him. From this time onwards there grew up a fierce and deadly rivalry between the two Churches. So intense was it that the actual names of the missions were forgotten and the Baganda referred to them by their national titles of 'Ba Ingreza' (English) and 'Ba Fransa' (French). Perhaps as a result of this constant bickering Mutesa was never converted to Christianity and died a pagan in 1884, whilst his son Mwanga became a Muslim. In 1885 Mwanga killed some of his young pages who had professed Christianity and in 1886 he martyred thirty more who refused to recant their faith, trussing them in straw mats and burning them alive.

The first cathedral on Namirembe Hill was a traditional Baganda building of wooden side walls and immense thatch roof; two other cathedrals were built on the site, then in 1913 work on the present cathedral was begun and in 1919 the impressive domed church was consecrated. One of the most pleasant things about Namirembe is that the faithful are called to prayer by African drums, not bells.

The Catholic Cathedral on Rubaga Hill was built by one lay brother with African help and it is a monument to his application and labour. The Romanesque front dominates the surroundings and the strong sunlight gives the building a modelling and definition that makes it stand out in bold relief. It is dedicated to the Martyrs who died in 1886 and who were beatified in 1920. As a result of the damage done to the two faiths by the identification of them with the nations who were their priests, the Catholics sent out an English order – the Mill Hill Fathers (St Joseph's) – and they set up their headquarters on Nsambya Hill.

The best known of the hills of Kampala is Makerere, site of the University and a pioneer in African education. It was founded in 1922 as a technical college, then in 1924 it started a medical school for Africans. In 1935 Sir Philip Mitchell became Governor of Uganda and at once saw the potential of Makerere for giving to Africans a full University education. The constitution of the board was changed so that it had representatives from all three territories sitting on it and the College gradually increased the scope of its courses and the standard of its teaching until in 1949 it became a college of the University of London. Now it is a University in its own right, with buildings better than many modern British Universities, a tree-shaded and beautiful campus and a driving determination to carry on the work of bringing higher education to as many as possible, to supply the desperate need for graduates in Africa.

75   Students relax on the campus of Makerere University

76   A print of 1875 showing
the seven hills of Kampala

The other hills of Kampala are Mulago which has the hospital, Kibuli with its mosque, a reminder that Islam came to Uganda before Christianity, and Nakasero covered with the modern shopping and business centre.

On Kasubi Hill stands the shrine of the dead Kabakas. It was always the tradition of the Baganda that a dead king was buried in his house, and when Mutesa died in 1884 his body was buried on the hill. Mwanga was exiled by the British Government to the Seychelles where he died in 1910. When his body was returned to Kampala for burial it posed a problem for he had no house to be buried in, so it was decided that he should be buried in the same place as his father Mutesa. When Mwanga's son Daudi Chwa died in 1939 the same problem arose, for by then the Kabaka had built himself a fine modern palace and it was not really possible for the tradition to be observed, so once again the entombment took place on Kasubi and the three generations sleep together. There is a great peace on Kasubi Hill. The tomb stands in the middle of a large clearing surrounded by the traditional palisade of grass.

77 The women from Kampala are known for their natural grace and sense of dress

Although built of modern materials the tomb itself is exactly the same as the original palace of the Kabakas. A great cone of thatch rises from the ground, on one side there is a low entrance flanked by stout wooden posts. Inside all is dark and there is a smell of thatch, bark cloth and woodsmoke. By each tomb stand the shields and spears, cloaks and ceremonial clothes used by the Kabaka, with his portrait by the side. On the ground are the pots and pans in use at the time of the Kabaka's death. The walls are draped with tapestries made of bark cloth and there are always attendants about the tombs. These are the 'wives' of the Kabakas who tend the tombs and the courtyard. The spiritual link between the Kabakas and the Baganda was always very strong and on Kasubi Hill the feelings of devotion and reverence are very apparent.

Because Kampala was so patently the royal town of Buganda it was necessary for the British to build their administrative centre elsewhere. They chose a small village on the shores of Lake Victoria nearly thirty miles from the capital. The decision to establish the seat of government at Entebbe was taken by Lord Portal, who had had experience of governing a state dominated by a strong ruler and who wished to dissociate himself from the local influence of the Baganda. He chose the name Entebbe for the place as it meant 'throne' but over the years the town grew to resemble nothing so much as an English garden suburb rather like Welwyn; it never lived up to its imperialistic name. Broad tree-shaded avenues, spacious houses hidden behind hedges of bougainvillaea and oleander, a total lack of bustle and urgency all added to the air of hieratic calm. No bustling African quarter or noisy bazaar area disturbed the peace in which senior Government officials moved majestically about their protocol-ridden lives. Entebbe, with its dignified and unpretentious Government House more like a country mansion than a palace, with its aloofness and introspective air, was a monument to the theories of indirect rule, the wise paternal direction standing above and beyond the day-to-day struggle of administration. So it stands today as obsolete and useless in the new Uganda as the policies for which it once stood.

It would be wrong to think of Kampala as a town of modern creation, for over two hundred years it has also been a thriving commercial centre. Arab traders first came to barter cloth for ivory and a whole host of local industries sprang up to tap the trade generated by the royal town. With the coming of the British, trade increased as the various companies developed the natural potential of the land. The staggering increase in the export of cotton and coffee has already been mentioned, but there were minerals such as copper at Kilembe; tea, hides and skins and animal feeding-stuffs for export; and large sugar production for consumption within East Africa. Because most of the land was in African hands the wealth created by this trade filtered rapidly down and so the African in Uganda enjoyed a very much higher standard of living than Africans in the neighbouring territories. Nowhere is this relative wealth more apparent than in Kampala. Round the bases of the main hills are a sea of African houses, their streets unplanned and running everyway, but with a standard of housing far above that of other capitals in East Africa. Cars jam the streets and everywhere one looks one sees the signs of wealth, the furniture for sale, the food in the shops, the appliances, the radios, the clothes.

The other impression that Kampala gives is its cleanliness; the houses are painted in gay colours and wherever one looks there are green spaces and trees. The air has a sparkle that is absent from the dust of Nairobi or the sullen humidity of Dar-es-Salaam and this sparkle gives a verve to the people that makes an immediate impact. The men move gracefully about the streets either dressed in western suits or the long white *kanzu* and tweed jacket that is almost a national costume. There seems to be less shouting and noise in the streets than in the other capitals and a more leisured tempo. But it is the women of Kampala who leave the most lasting impression on one. Tall and dignified, with lovely high cheek-bones and fine-drawn faces, they walk about the city with a grace and beauty unrivalled in any other capital in the world. Allied to their beauty of form is an innate dress sense that shows itself in the colours of their long dresses, always harmonious and never garish; the poise and pride of many generations of breeding are inherent in their progress along the bright streets.

Because of its long history as a royal town Kampala has the greatest adjustment of all the capitals to make. The traditional divisions within the city are hard to break down and the very fact that each area had its own focus on its own hilltop gave the city a parochialism that has been difficult to overcome. The division between the Baganda and the other tribes who are now flocking into the city is very real, and with the dethronement of the Kabaka the Baganda feel hemmed in and overpowered. These tensions are very real and can only be resolved by a long process of contact and mutual understanding. The time has been woefully short to prepare the city, so traditional in its conceptions, to take its place as the capital of one of the new nations of Africa.

Mombasa and Nairobi are really twin towns, or even a single town with its two halves 320 miles apart but linked very firmly by modern communications. This is not really as fanciful as it sounds for Nairobi grew from Mombasa and then took over the seat of government leaving Mombasa as the port and maritime business centre. The two towns are inter-dependent, each fulfilling a part but needing the other for completion.

The foundation of Mombasa is lost in the dim legends of the past – it has been identi-fied with the Egyptian *Land of Punt* and with the *Rhapta* of Ptolemy. What is certain is the fact that it was a port in the days of the first Arab penetrations of the Coast. The natural advantages of the harbour must have been apparent to the earliest navigators, for Mombasa is built on an island with deep water both to the north and the south. It is composed of coral and is, in fact, a coral atoll that has grown in the centre of what was once a lagoon with a narrow entrance from the sea. To the west the island was connected to the mainland by a ford, and it is here that a causeway was built to link it to the mainland. The importance of Mombasa in early days is confirmed by its name, which is a Swahili corruption from the Arabic *Ma nabas*, the place of public speaking (i.e. a place of assembly and debate).

The Portuguese found Mombasa a large and prosperous town with a high wall around it and the harbour filled with trading dhows. The houses were not the usual mud hovels, they were 'many storied' and jammed together in narrow streets. There was a subsidiary village to the south of the island overlooking the harbour called Kilindini ('the deep water'). This was used as an anchorage during the north-east monsoons as it was sheltered from them by the island.

The Portuguese built a town by the northern harbour, and started the fortifications that culminated in the building of Fort Jesus. The sieges and tribulations of the Fort have been told in Chapter 2; but even after the defeat of the Portuguese there was constant war in Mombasa. The island was dominated by a whole succession of chiefs and Governors until the coming of the Imperial British East Africa Company, whose primary area of influence was Uganda. It was fertile and obviously worthy of commercial exploitation and where there were strong kings able to make binding treaties which they could enforce. Mombasa therefore became the headquarters of the Company, but it lay at the end of a long and hazardous journey from its main sphere of activity and it was obvious that some speedy means of communication must be found between the port and its hinterland. The first pro-posal was a road for animal transport, but it soon became clear that a railway was what was really required. The Imperial Company in 1890 tried to get Government help to cover the interest on the capital needed for the work but for some years the granting of this aid was postponed, mainly due to the Liberal Opposition in Parliament who were very anti-colonial. The Company, however, started the survey for the line on its own initiative in 1891. In December 1895 Mr (later Sir George) Whitehouse, an engineer who had built railways in South Africa, South America and India, landed in Mombasa to take over the construction of the line. Indentured Indian coolie labour was to be used to construct the line as it was thought the local Africans would take too long to teach, and the first batch arrived in January 1896. The actual engineering difficulties of the line were formidable, for as soon as it crossed to the mainland it was faced by a climb through the coastal hills, and then a long haul through undulating country with ridges running at right angles to the line,

78   Mombasa Island. The old harbour with the dense mass of
Arab houses is on the right of the island, before the bridge. On
the left is the modern city with the port of Kilindini at the top left

so that cuttings and embankments of over forty-five feet were common. Progress was therefore very slow, but in 1898 work was held up for a completely different reason. Two man-
eating lions appeared near Tsavo and started to terrorise the labour gangs. For over nine
months these lions appeared to wage a personal war against the railway. They seemed to
have supernatural cunning in evading traps, poison bait and bullets, going to any lengths
to obtain their diet of human beings. The coolies were firmly convinced of the lions' magical
origin, saying that they were the spirits of two chiefs come to prevent the railway entering
African land. So great did their depredations become that for three weeks all work came to a
complete standstill. Finally, after a long and most exciting hunt, they were shot by Colonel
J. H. Patterson, the engineer in charge of the Tsavo section. They had by that time killed
over a hundred people.

The trouble with man-eaters continued and for a long while the railway paid a bounty
of 200 rupees (£15) for every lion shot in the railway zone. Perhaps the most daring of all
the killings happened in June 1900. Mr Ryall, the Railway Police Superintendent, was
travelling with two European traders when he was told that there was a man-eater at Kima
station. All three hunted for it during the day and sat up for the first part of the night in the
inspection carriage. Feeling tired they then lay down, the two traders on the lower bunks
and Ryall on the upper. The carriage doors were of the sliding variety and somehow the

79  Nairobi in 1900. The first buildings were wooden framed with corrugated-iron roofs. In the foreground is a tented encampment made by settlers waiting for their allocations of land

80  An early shop in Nairobi comprising general store, hotel and bar. The heat generated in the corrugated-iron bar must have been excellent for trade!

lion managed to force one back. It stood with its forepaws on the chest of the trader in the lower bunk while it grabbed Ryall. Then, with Ryall in its mouth, it jumped through a window and escaped into the bush. This lion was subsequently trapped and put on show for the benefit of the coolies before being killed. Despite these difficulties the rails reached Nairobi in June 1899 – three years after plate laying started at Mombasa.

The siting of Nairobi was almost fortuitous, there was certainly no idea of its eventual growth into the capital city. Before the railroad came, a road had been cut inland from Mombasa to take the trade and traffic to Uganda. The first part of the road was called Mackinnon Road (in honour of the founder of the Imperial British East Africa Company), and reached as far as Kibwezi. From there a second road was made by Captain B. Sclater of the Royal Engineers who cut it from Kibwezi across the Athi Plains to Kikuyu and then down into the Kedong River valley. The actual site of Nairobi was picked by one of Sclater's men, a Sergeant Ellis, who made it a depot for stores on the open plains near fresh water. Thus of all the capitals of East Africa, Nairobi is the only one that was founded by Europeans with no roots in the African past.

Nairobi was an ideal site for a temporary railhead as it was the last flat land before the steep climb to the Kikuyu escarpment and the much steeper descent into the Rift Valley. Here the railway engineers could lay out their stores, build sidings, running sheds, watering points, turntables and engineering shops. However suitable as a halting place on the long haul to Uganda it is doubtful if it is the best possible site for the capital, lying as it does on the plains, dry and scorched during the hot weather when dust devils dance in the heat shimmer, impassable with thick black mud during the rains. But, once railhead had been established, the possibility of changing the site of the capital to the cooler heights round Limuru was lost.

The first township that grew up round the railway did not last very long. Colonel Patterson, who was by then Divisional Engineer, gives the whole story in his usual terse but vivid style. 'Wonderfully soon, however, the nucleus of the present town began to take shape, and a thriving bazaar sprang into existence with a mushroom-like growth. In this, however, a case or two of plague broke out before very long, so I gave the natives and Indians who inhabited it an hour's notice to clear out, and on my own responsibility promptly burned the whole place to the ground.'

From this beginning the town developed gradually. There was a small General Store operated by a firm called Boustead and Ridley which sold everything, a small corrugated-iron hotel and a few mud-and-wattle Indian shops. The early bungalows were built on the bluff overlooking the railway workshops, named Whitehouse Hill after the Chief Engineer. Gradually the pattern of the town began to emerge – a long road from the railway out towards the St Austin's Mission, already established on the higher ground to the west, and branching from this another leading out to Dagoretti Village and Fort Smith, the original post set up in the Kikuyu lands. It was, in fact, the first building in East Africa constructed with burnt bricks. Upon these two axes, Government Road and Delamere Avenue (now called Kenyatta Avenue), the rest of the town grew and began to fill in the spaces.

Government Road became the main shopping centre and Delamere Avenue the centre for hotels, banks and auction yards for stock and goods, so it was to Delamere Avenue that the settlers first came when they visited Nairobi to buy their supplies and stock for their farms. In those early days the only means of transport was by a trek cart drawn by a span of sixteen oxen, so buildings along either side of the Avenue were set wide enough apart to allow for the turning of these long spans. This distance was maintained when new buildings were put up and the modern Nairobi dweller has reason to bless this accident of transport that has given him one of the widest and most handsome of avenues.

Between the wars there was steady growth as the economy gradually expanded, bringing more businessmen and officials to the capital. European housing spread along the Muthaiga Ridge, a pleasant well-treed area. Then, as the pressure for land mounted, the suburb of Karen was developed. This had been the farm and coffee estate of the Countess Karen von Blixen, lying on the edge of the Masai Reserve under the Ngong Hills that she loved. She is perhaps better known as the writer Isak Dinesen, but under her proper name she wrote *Out of Africa*, a book of deep perception and love that is surely one of the most moving of the accounts of early settler life. For its expanding Indian and Goanese staff the Railway built houses at Eastleigh (named after the large locomotive and wagon sheds near South-ampton) and the Africans spilt out from Kariakor, originally built as barracks for the Carrier Corps of porters used in the East African campaign, to new locations to the north and east.

It is the last twenty years, since the end of the war, that have seen the real change in Nairobi. A change that has taken a dirty, rather squalid town and made it into an inter-national capital with tall office blocks, hotels, shops and restaurants, new housing for all races, fine new legislative and municipal buildings, an international airport and a University. The city (for it was given its Royal Charter in 1950) has triumphantly turned its position on the flat plain to advantage and the new high buildings shine in the harsh sunlight, their sides etched with black shadows from balconies and buttresses. Nairobi is a city of colour. Not only the primary colours of cladding set off by the white concrete of the new buildings, but also the profusion of trees and flowers. The jacarandas, with a flower as blue as a harebell, that cover Delamere Avenue with a carpet of fallen blooms, the city parks that are a mass of bougainvillaea, the private gardens that riot with blooms. Of all of these the greatest triumph is the Princess Elizabeth Highway – now called Uhuru (Freedom) Highway – a dual carriage-way ring-road that must be the most gardened highway in the world. The City Parks Department under the direction of Mr Greensmith took an ordinary stretch of roadway and turned it into a magic drive through coloured shrubs and trees. There are great fountains of bougainvillaea drifting from large tripods, or making a solid wall of colour along the roadside fences, or standing as specimens, their heads a tight ball of red, yellow or purple. There are bottle-brush trees, their strange red flowers contrasting with yellow *grevillea* and *mimosa*. The roundabouts are rock gardens of succulents and aloes, or lilies and shrubs; each one different, fitting its landscape; each one a *tour de force* of the gardener's craft.

Although Nairobi has no roots in the past of Africa, she has preserved a part of her heritage within a few minutes of the city centre. The plain on which the city is built was once the haunt of hundreds of species of game; wildebeeste and zebra trampled over the first settlers' flower beds, buck and gazelle ate their roses, hyenas scavenged their dustbins, leopards killed their dogs and cats. Even fifteen years ago zebra used to break into the

81   Nairobi in 1961. In the background are the Ngong Hills.
Kenyatta Avenue is the broad thoroughfare on the right of the
picture. In the foreground is the modern housing that has replaced
the old African shanty town

82　Parliament Building, Nairobi

airport to graze between the runways, and lions were seen in suburban gardens. Before it was too late the Kenya National Park created the Nairobi Park, an area where the inhabitants and visitors could drive and watch game with no barriers and the minimum of restriction. The sides of the park bounding the urban area were strongly fenced, but to the south and west the park was open to the plains, so that the animals move into and out of the area as they will. It is a park absolutely unique in conception and realisation, a zoological garden which is really that – no bars, no cages, where the animals are free to come and go and only the humans are confined, where lions kill and eat oblivious to the ring of watchers in their cars. The whole spirit of the enterprise is summed up in the words of dedication written by King George VI –

'The wild life of today is not ours to dispose of as we please, we have it on trust, we must account for it to those who come after.'

It is perhaps appropriate that it is Nairobi, the city with no roots in the past, that should lead in the struggle to find a new way of life for the mixture of peoples who now live in East Africa. Maybe, from this improbably sited city, with its brash new buildings set in a plain where the dust devils still spiral skywards and zebra graze unaffected by the roar of jets, where the raw colours of nature clash and scream in the heat, will come a new stability and prosperity that will show the way for the rest of the continent.

# Conclusion

ELSPETH HUXLEY once compared writing about East Africa to drawing a galloping horse; before you have started, the horse is over the horizon. In writing this book I have felt rather like a painter asked to make a detailed portrait of an elephant on a postage stamp, the sheer size of the subject dwarfs the medium.

There is so much more that I should have liked to put in; so much that has had to be left out through lack of space. East Africa is a land of contrasts; of snow on the equator; of clear, ice-cold water bubbling out of dusty lava rock; of Arabic remains and modern ports; of barren deserts and lush savannah lands; of old tribal customs and modern politics; where you can grow daffodils and pineapples on the same farm, catch trout and crocodiles in the same river. It has a history that stretches back to the beginnings of man and a mixture of peoples who are only just learning to understand one another.

By studying the history, the people and the land in which they live, it may be that the problems that face East Africa will be more comprehensible to those who watch this area with interest and hope. Pliny's tag *Ex Africa semper aliquid novi* is as true as ever. Out of East Africa may be coming the new pattern of coexistence between the three races of the world; where African, Asian and European are equal citizens of one country, bound together by a common franchise, working together for a common future.

# Acknowledgements

I SHOULD LIKE TO THANK Mrs Elizabeth Adcock for transforming my appalling manuscript into typescript; Mrs Maureen Johnston for drawing the maps and diagrams; and Miss Jennifer Smith for reading the proofs. I should also like to thank Messrs Wallace Heaton for their care and patience in producing prints, and the library of the old East African High Commission for much help with photographs and information, before it was disbanded.

C. P. K.

THE AUTHOR AND PUBLISHERS wish to record their grateful thanks to copyright owners for use of the illustrations listed below:

To Aerofilms Limited for: 2, 53, 68, 69, 70, 78.

To the Imperial War Museum for: 22, 23, 24, 25.

To the Kenya High Commissioner for: 28, 29, 57, 58, 81, 82.

To the Royal Geographical Society for: 12, 13, 14, 15, 16, 17, 18, 19, 20, 21, 76, 79, 80.

To the Tanzania High Commissioner for: 11, 26, 40, 46, 48, 56, 59, 67.

To the Uganda High Commissioner for: 27, 51, 52, 75.

All other photographs are from the author's collection.

# Index

NOTE. *In Swahili the correct prefix for a people is* Wa, *for example the Gogo are correctly* Wagogo, *they live in* Ugogo *and they speak* Kigogo; *but in making the index I have ignored these niceties and indexed the people without prefix (*Kikuyu *not* Wakikuyu*) unless the prefix has become part of the anglicised name, e.g. Baganda not* Ganda

*Printed in Great Britain by Jarrold & Sons Limited, Norwich*